OPERATING BUDGETS

Operating Budgets

WILLIAM J. VATTER

University of California, Berkeley

WADSWORTH PUBLISHING COMPANY, INC.
BELMONT, CALIFORNIA

L. C. Cat. Card No.: 77–96286

Printed in the United States of America

1 2 3 4 5 6 7 8 9 10—74 73 72 71 70 69

PREFACE

Operating Budgets is intended as a general introduction to the field of managerial accounting. It should help build a foundation for the study of cost analysis and standards, the relations between statistics and accounting control, and the expansion of ideas about control procedures, long-run planning, and the nature and content of information systems. But whether or not the book is used in those ways, its basic purpose is to present in compact form those management and accounting ideas that make budgets work.

Budgets bring into play practically all the managerial skills and tools, because budgets are a systematic approach to planning and control techniques at every level of organization. Historically, budgetary control developed as an adjunct to financial control through accounting records and reports; but however much it may have grown in content and sophistication, it is still directed toward the results that are measured by accounting data and financial statements.

Thus, we base the study of budgets upon a modest familiarity with accounting, such as might be had from a typical first course. However, there is no need for much technical emphasis, for this book is concerned mostly with why budgets are used and how they function. Of course, there are places where someone with special interests or skills (statistics, mathematical models, or an interest in behavioral problems) might undertake excursions from the main stream of thought with satisfaction and profit. But all such things cannot be encompassed in a small and introductory volume.

I would like to thank R. Lee Brummet, of the University of Michigan, and Robert H. Gregory, the editor of the Wadsworth Accounting Series, for their helpful comments on the manuscript of this book. Any possible errors or omissions are, of course, mine alone.

CONTENTS

1

MANAGEMENT'S INTEREST IN BUDGETS

Accounting ideas are used in many ways to assist and promote good management. One of these is budgetary control of operations, or more simply, the use of operating budgets. In this book we will try to uncover the basic ideas and techniques that are useful in budgetary control to show how budgets are prepared and how management uses them. To do this we will need to develop some ideas about management and to expand some notions about the collection and use of accounting information. Since accounting and management are closely intertwined in budgetary processes, it will not always be easy to be sure that we are talking about one or the other, and we shall not try to separate management ideas from accounting operations. This is, however, as it should be; accounting measurements and reports ought to be closely related to the uses which they are to serve.

Budgets are management tools that are tied in to accounting operations in many ways, and we will have to observe these things a few at a time, piecemeal. But it will help if we have at least a general notion of what budgets have to do with management and accounting. We can begin this by observing that management is decision making; decisions are choices between alternative plans or forecasts, and these forecasts can be based on accounting as well as other data and considerations.

DECISIONS

An enterprise is a group of people that works with selected tools or facilities to produce some wanted product or service. These people must work together if they are to achieve the aim of the enterprise. They must agree, or at least be willing, to do whatever is needed in whatever way is the best way to achieve the desired results. This raises a number of questions: What results are desired? What methods are to be used? Who is to do what, and when? The answers to such questions are decisions, and the task of managers is to seek the proper answers to questions about the kinds and amounts of products or services the firm will produce, how these will be provided and sold, where and how the various personal, technical, and financial resources will be acquired—all of the thousand-and-one issues that must be resolved if the people, ideas, equipment, and other resources are to work together for a common purpose. The processes of decision making are the central element in management.

The Nature of Decisions

A decision is usually stated as a flat assertion of an order or a plan —some course of action that is to be pursued. But the real content of a decision lies in the way in which that result is achieved. Sometimes we decide passively—we do nothing and let things happen as they may. At other times we make decisions capriciously or arbitrarily, basing our choices on feelings, attitudes, habits, or whims. As long as the decision is personal and does not involve extensive resources, passive or capricious decision making may be harmless. But when a decision affects many people or involves large amounts of resources, decision making must be careful and logical.

As a logical process, decision making is somewhat complex, but it has three quite easily recognized features. First, it is oriented toward the future; we cannot decide what has already transpired. Second, decision making involves the consideration of some set of alternatives; a situation from which there can be only one outcome or only one way to deal with it permits no decision. Third, there must be some way to rank or evaluate the outcomes expected from the various alternatives. Making a decision logically requires that in dealing with the future, we identify all feasible courses of action and rate them to determine which is best suited for the objectives involved.

The need for logical decision making in management arises from the number of people and the amount of resources which may be affected. A decision made without a real effort to forecast consequences is arbitrary and reckless, and it may work havoc when its effects are widespread. Yet in order to simplify administration, the decision process may be short-circuited by the use of standing rules or procedures. These are the result of analysis and decision at some earlier time; their continued use avoids restudy and redecision, which can be a waste of time and effort. For instance, we may set a decision rule for quality inspection in terms of the number of defective units in a prescribed sample or a decision rule in the use of maximum or minimum size specifications for parts. These rules are based upon a previous analysis in which the evaluations have been made in general terms, but the use of the rule assumes the correctness of that analysis.

The Use of Data in Decision Making

Managers need to make "good" decisions; they need to be right in their forecasts if they are to remain managers for very long. Basing decisions on guesses—however shrewd—is not as safe an approach as using numerical data from past experience to forecast future expectations. If a worker turns out 30 units of product per hour under given conditions, it is reasonable to expect this to be repeated or extended. To produce 150 units, five hours would be required. Because numerical data are positive, objective, and easy to extend or apply, they are helpful in forecasting.

Analysis

Merely having data from which to forecast is not always enough to insure correct results. One needs to be sure that the extrapolation can be depended upon—that there is no unnoticed factor that might upset the forecast. A worker turning out 30 units of product per hour uses tools and equipment whose condition has much to do with the worker's performance; the materials used, the methods of handling things, conditions in the work environment, as well as the worker's attitudes, feelings, and skills all affect the results. Hence we need some assurance that these contributing variables are identified and that the conditions are maintained or allowed for in the forecast. "Feedback," checking expectations against actual results, serves to show whether or not distorting factors have affected the validity of forecasts.

Feedback as an Accounting Function

One of the most important accounting functions is to measure the results that follow decisions; comparing these results with the plan indicates how successfully the plan was carried out. This kind of comparison is an effective way to check the entire managerial process. A difference between expectations and results means one of two things: either the forecast on which the decision was based was in error, or those responsible for carrying out the decision have somehow failed to do as was expected. In either case, some action is indicated. If the plan was wrong, it should be changed. If the plan was right but the operations were not properly carried out, communication or operating methods need improvement.

This process may continue over several stages. Suppose someone has decided how a certain product should be packed. This decision may have been quite arbitrary and unscientific when the problem was first dealt with. Then a package of this product becomes damaged in shipment. The reason may be that someone failed to follow the instructions in packing. But it may also mean that the design of the package (or the method of packing) is not adequate or well thought out. Study of the damage and investigation of how packing is actually done will usually indicate whether the plan or its execution was deficient. If there is no reason to question the validity of the plan, we may try first to make sure the work was done properly. If the execution cannot be improved, the plan must be changed. But then it may happen that although no damage occurs, the costs of packing are higher than they were expected to be; this may be because of using too much packing material or too much time in making certain that the package was safe. The same approach is again used; either the plan or the execution was at fault. Over a period of time, feedback may be used to initiate improvements that will ultimately solve the problem.

It should be stressed that merely observing differences is not enough to solve problems; there must be some kind of analysis and interpretation to be able to effect improvements. Suppose the expected output from a given activity is 30 units per hour. We may follow the operations from hour to hour, discovering each time we check some other reason for trouble. There may be dull or otherwise inadequate tools; unsatisfactory working conditions in the way of lighting, ventilation, or work place; poor material; improper or inadequate instructions or worker training; carelessness; or fatigue. These conditions are the things that affect the cost. Only by analysis is it possible to get hold of the factors that cause trouble and that can be controlled. Budgetary control is based on this approach, because this is the underlying nature of managerial activities—the essential content of the managerial process. The use of accounting procedures to provide data for managerial plans as well as to check on their effectiveness is a vital part of overall management.

Feedback as Systematic Control

The ideas that have been presented may be applied to the entire range of management problems. Planning always underlies the making of decisions, and plans are based on forecasts. Having made a decision and given orders which will implement the chosen plan, managers rely upon accounting or other reports to control operations. If actual events conform to expectations, both the planning and the performance are assumed to be satisfactory. If results of decisions do not work out as they are expected to, some form of adjustment is in order. This may be extended into what is called a "principle of exceptions"; that is, managers do not concern themselves with opera-

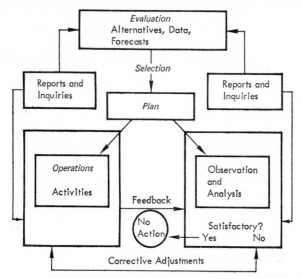

Figure 1–1. *The feedback control system*

tions that are proceeding according to plan—only the exceptions call for attention. The operations of a business may thus be reduced to a number of routines or subsystems of control, each of which could be fitted to a diagram something like that in Figure 1–1.

This system of feedback control starts with an evaluation of the task to be done. The plan of operation is chosen from alternatives, using forecasts based at least partially on accounting data. Orders to put this plan into effect go to those concerned with implementation —doing what the plan calls for—but another copy of each order is sent to an observation center (controller's division, standards department, accounting or statistical control office). This copy informs the observation center of management's expectations, for later comparison with actual results. Operations and activities result in a steady flow of feedback information to the observation-analysis center. So long as these data about operations fall within a tolerable range of expected results, no action is taken. But when deviations exceed acceptable limits, the operators are alerted, so that needed adjustments will not be overlooked.

As a matter of routine, however, a steady stream of reports delivers information to managers. The decision makers are thus aware of overall results, and most of their routine questions will be answered from these reports. When changes in the operation are considered, the routine reports will provide a basis for planning and forecasting. But when problems arise, it may be necessary to request additional or special data, and there should be some easy way to raise questions and receive additional information. This is provided in the model by an informal inquiry-response channel to handle the flow of supplementary data, in either direction, between decision makers and the operators.

The notion of feedback control is a common one in mechanical and electrical systems, such as speed governors, temperature controls, automatic carburetion, and electric current and power transmission devices. As applied to management operations, it maintains operations and activities within planned limits in all areas. Inventories, production, sales, receivables, and personnel and machine performance afford many illustrations of feedback control.

The Continuing Necessity of Reporting

It should be stressed that the feedback control system does not make regular reports any less valuable. It is necessary to maintain a regular reporting system, not only to provide general information when questions arise, but also to be able to judge the effectiveness of any one operation against the overall enterprise aims. For instance, a feedback control may serve to keep the costs of producing a product close to plan, and a similar arrangement may keep the sales program within close tolerance to the planned results. But minor changes in sales prices may call for adjustments in production schedules and costs to meet the shift in market conditions. There is also a need to make sure that the amount of variance from plan, which may be small enough to go unnoticed from day to day, does not cumulate over a period to make the overall result unsatisfactory.

Further, it should be noted that a mere reporting of differences does not establish what caused them. There ought to be a careful attempt to see *why* certain things happen, so that their reoccurrence may be avoided. We shall have occasion to see this when we discuss the processes of review and revision of budget plans and the procedures that are related to budget enforcement.

VARIOUS KINDS OF BUSINESS PLANS

Until now, our discussion of management decisions has been general. We have not paid attention to the fact that there are several different kinds of planning that managers must do. Every enterprise exhibits some kind of a hierarchy of plans; some are very broad and comprehensive, others are less so. We shall gain perspective if we examine some of the major classes of management plans.

Objectives

The objectives of an enterprise are long-range, overall plans which underlie and govern the whole structure and operation of the company. They are the basic aims toward which the company's entire existence is geared; objectives set out the boundaries for all subordinate plans. A company's objectives are more specific than the mere hope of making a profit; they indicate its area of operations, specify its expected size and scope, and define its economic functions—the services or products in which the company intends to specialize. Objectives deal with long-term issues. What we do in this year must be established with careful regard to what we hope to do ultimately. A company can maintain logical continuity of operations only by following its long-range objectives.

A company may have as an objective the production and sale of a full line of electrical home appliances, even though it may at this time be making only washing machines and dryers. But management must have before it a clear idea of what other products it hopes to develop and how these products should be related to one another. There ought to be some plan about how far and how intensively the company will try to develop its market—geographically, in terms of the class of customers to be sought out, and the ultimate scope of market coverage. Setting goals of this kind builds a frame or a basis for other decisions; an electric home appliance company would not be likely to start producing watches or automobiles. The skills and facilities which a company brings together must be selected to meet certain purposes; they will not generally serve many other ones. Therefore, objectives must be established carefully, because they tend to set up the company as an institution, with definite characteristics and capabilities.

This does not mean, of course, that a company may never change its goals; it may sometimes be necessary to change them. When the market for a company's line of products declines or disappears, management must re-examine the objectives of the firm that have become unattainable because of the shift. A company that has been unsuccessful in the manufacture of automobiles could be expected to shift over into other fields where it might hope to do a better job. A company that has been producing freight-car wheels and frames for the railroads might want to shift its sights when competition from trucking companies begins to affect its customers. An oil producing and refining company ought to consider what it will do if solar energy can be used to drive vehicles or if it becomes possible to transmit electric energy by radio waves. Projections like these may seem a bit farfetched, but successful companies do make a positive effort to keep aware of such possibilities in making their long-range plans. Specifying the objectives of a company and considering what changes may be required to keep the company aimed in the right direction set the tone and the course for the whole enterprise.

Policies

Given a certain pattern of objectives, a company will make other plans which serve as general guides as to how it will deal with various situations. Such plans are called policies; they represent attitudes or viewpoints which the company tries consistently to maintain in all its operations. For example, the company may adopt a policy of diversification in products—a decision to avoid concentration on only one or a few product lines. This might be its way of implementing its aim of reducing the effects of cyclical fluctuations. In an extreme example, a company might not only produce machines and supplies related to agricultural production, but also have a large chemical products division, as well as units that make and sell prestressed concrete beams, industrial pumps, special equipment designed for oil-well drilling operations, and some specialized types of military vehicles.

A company may have a policy on its rate of financial expansion or a recognized aversion to the use of debt securities in raising funds. Many of our large companies have grown by reinvestment of earnings rather than by new security issues. Policies are distinguished from objectives by their more specific nature and by the fact that they represent the company position on certain pervasive and continuing problems. Policies are changed more frequently than objectives, but they are changed only for very important reasons; a consistent and coherent set of attitudes toward problems and conditions is essential to a company's success.

Strategies

Strategies are plans for dealing with specific problems or programs of a short-range nature, usually to implement long-range objectives within the constraints of established policy. The way in which a new product is launched or the kind of approach that is taken to implement advertising under a given set of conditions are examples of strategies. A chemical company with an objective of becoming one of the leaders in its field (in size, progressiveness, research, and quality) may set up a policy of product diversification in order to develop intensively the uses of certain basic materials. One of these products may be polyethylene plastic, and the company may promote the use of this product to replace paper in certain kinds of mailing containers; the selection of potential customers, the kind of appeals made, and the media used would be strategy decisions. A department store might establish branches in certain satellite cities under a policy of controlled expansion, but it may choose to centralize its patterns of buying and its decisions about merchandise price lines and inventories. A shirt manufacturer might try to acquire the plants of smaller manufacturers who are retiring from business and use them for its own production, thus taking advantage of lower investments and favorable labor conditions in smaller cities. Strategies are plans of some breadth, but they are less permanent, and they deal with more specialized and detailed problems than do policies or objectives.

Procedures

As the kinds of plans we consider become more short-run and even more specialized in nature, they tend to raise questions that recur; these questions could be answered by establishing procedures, or standard methods. These procedures might be subject to frequent and minor changes (as opposed to the less frequent and more far-reaching aspects of strategies, policies, and longer term decisions), but they are set up in considerably more detail. At the extreme, there are "standard instructions" for performing such clerical tasks as filing, checking, or filling out forms, and there are lists of the steps required to operate certain machines or tools.

PLANS CLASSIFIED BY SUBJECT MATTER

We have been discussing business plans without giving very much attention to the way in which they may vary in subject matter, because our concern has been to stress the various *levels* of plans.

These range from the broad and general, relatively permanent objectives and policies to the narrow and specific but shorter lived strategies and procedures. This is one dimension of the planning task. As we shall see, this permits a kind of specialization in management, for if one can set up really effective policies to make sure that overall goals are properly approached, the task of working out strategic and procedural plans may become less difficult, and it may be given to other people to work out. This process of delegation is an aspect of organization, the management structure employed to systematize decision making.

Plans do, however, have special import for different subject areas. There are decisions, for instance, that affect the relations among workers; the way in which the company goes about recruiting potential employees, and the tests that are applied to measure the progress of workers, or to assign them to particular tasks are specialized questions, the answers to which are usually worked out by personnel officers. On the other hand, there are technological problems that must be worked out to deal with machines, materials, and specifications. These may range from the design of products, plants, and processes to various aspects of scheduling and routing the manufacturing operations. They may involve the number of items and kinds of inventory to be maintained by purchasing and receiving techniques; they may have to do with the degree of product standardization—the number of sizes, colors, and finishes to be handled or the kind of product or process inspection to be maintained.

It should be noted that the classification of plans by subject matter is separate from their breadth of view, or time dimension. Plans for product standardization, the maintenance of a "price leadership" in the sales market, operating according to a seniority system, or maintaining a "union shop" may be strategic problems, or even policy-level issues. Thus, we have two dimensions of planning that may operate together. Plans that concern a certain subject matter may be of narrow or broad scope; decisions at a given level may affect various subject matters. This gives us a chance to make management itself more efficient, through the kind of specialization called administrative organization.

ORGANIZATION STRUCTURES

The fact that plans encompass such wide diversity, calling for the exercise of different skills and viewpoints, makes it advisable to work out a plan for making decisions. This is a systematic pattern of relationships among the various managers who operate in different parts of the business. By making up this pattern, we can indicate who will make certain kinds of decisions, both in terms of the level and the subject matter involved. Since the hierarchy of plans involves a degree of consistency and dependence, the organization will be set up in the same fashion. Charts will show which decisions are subordinate to others and, thus, which managers should report to or "work under" those who have broader responsibilities. Even in a modestly small firm there will be a fairly large number of decisions to be made; these will fall into various jurisdictional areas. Which customers will be called on this week will be decided by the salesmen, but how big a sales territory should be, and how intensively it should be worked, could be better judged by a district sales manager. A broader question, such as what *kinds* of customers should be sought, may involve certain aspects of credit extension which concern both the sales and finance divisions as a matter of policy.

When we talk about product design, other viewpoints and interests must be considered. The people who produce the product will not be the ones who sell it. Production plans and decisions may be approached in terms of maintaining enough volume to get economy in plant utilization. Having a large number of sizes, colors, types, and other variations in products may mean higher costs, greater inventories, and more detail in planning production. Yet the sales division may think that such variety is essential for customer satisfaction and high sales volume. Different views on such matters must be resolved. Whether a given product should be produced or promoted in certain ways may require a policy decision on the scope or range of products, outlining a position on the amount of variety in size, color, and other product characteristics. Product policy involves not only the sales division's idea of appropriate market approaches, customer service, and price ranges, but also the product division's notions about technical problems of product design, selection of processes, equipment, and methods; the policy adopted will have implications for financial structure and financing transactions, and there may be personnel problems associated with the production volume and steady work in the plant. Product policy may involve research and development activities, tax and legal questions; such a broad array of angles requires participation of a number of managers in making decisions. The need for some orderly process of decision making makes it desirable to set up an arrangement to recognize the various tasks and abilities involved. This kind of jurisdictional structure is a systematic framework to facilitate decision making, which is portrayed in an organization chart like that in Figure 1–2.

In this organization chart only the production function is carried out to show much detail; the personnel and engineering sections are specified only in general terms, and the sales and finance functions are merely noted to indicate some of the major issues given attention. Nevertheless, the chart gives a fair idea of how various activities and decisions concerning them are assigned to the jurisdiction of a number of managers.

A company organization chart is important not only as a plan for assigning responsibility to a number of managers for the making of specified decisions, but also for other reasons. Organization charts may serve as indicators of formal communication channels; they show who "takes orders from" or "gives orders to" other persons or who "reports to" whom. The chart may indicate something of the line of promotion; it may also show a social or a political hierarchy. There are many relationships and contacts between managers that cannot be shown on the organization chart; the personal relationships and the various kinds of decision-making power are only imperfectly shown. But it is useful to have some means to describe the way in which the task of decision making is spread among managers. As we will see, that set of plans we call a budget is prepared and enforced by the various managers whose positions are reflected in the organization chart. These managers divide the budget task in much the same way as the regular operations are structured.

Measuring Units

One other aspect of managerial planning must be considered before we can visualize clearly what a budget is; we need to pay some attention to the units that are used to set up plans. Plans can cover many different things. One can plan for the attitudes, feelings, and behavior of people or for the physical dimensions and characteristics of a product. If a given electrical circuit is to achieve a desired magnetic or mechanical effect, we may plan in electrical units (volts, ohms, amperes), in mechanical units (pounds, inches, pressures, speeds) or some combination, so as to program different aspects of the overall plan. But financial units can be used in a wide range of situations, and we may try to express a whole program in one set of units. To gain simplicity and coherence, budgets are set up this way; the varied statistical measures used to work out parts of a plan are summarized in an overall program expressed in money units.

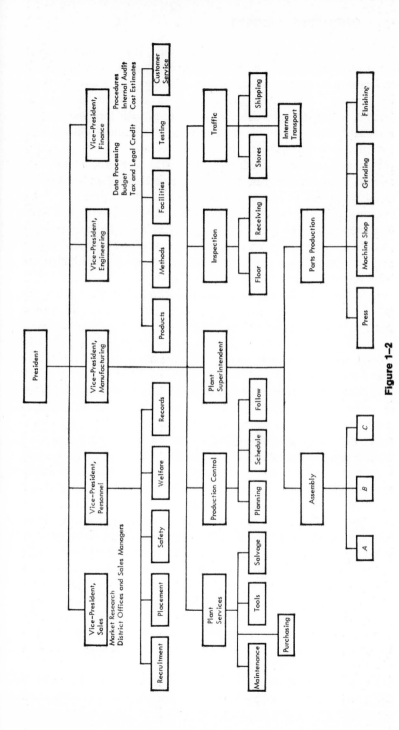

Figure 1-2

The expression of budgets in money units is sometimes taken to mean that budgets deal with receipt and payment of cash. This is understandable, for personal budgets are, typically, plans for "handling money." That is, we plan spending to stay within the limits of income, which for individuals is the same as cash receipts. Thus, a personal budget is often viewed as a plan for spending—setting forth how much is to be paid out, when, and to whom.

Part of business budgeting is, of course, concerned with cash receipts and payments. But the business budget is not limited by cash income. Business firms can borrow more and oftener than individuals can, and they may also finance operations from the investments made by shareholders, who are primarily interested in having their equity in the firm increase as a result of productive and profitable operations of the firm. But business budgets are different from personal budgets in other respects as well.

In a business, the processes of production and sale are complicated; they involve the use of many skills and services and various kinds of equipment, as well as prerequisites such as patents, copyrights, or trade secrets, besides ordinary materials and supplies. The flow of various economic services in the business firm is difficult to follow and to measure.

In addition, businesses do not consume things as people do. Much of our personal expenditures are for food, shelter, or comforts; to these we do not ordinarily apply very objective standards. As people we do not try to be really efficient in our choices or consumption of food, housing, automobiles, electric blankets, or other things we buy. We choose on less logical, more personal grounds. However, a business must match input against output to be sure that what is produced is actually worth (will recover) what it costs. Although it is just as easy (maybe easier!) to waste business resources as it is to squander personal assets, we do not apply the same standards. Personal satisfaction may justify outlays that in a business firm would be waste; an individual may enjoy his extravagance, but inefficient business operations create no pleasure to justify their cost. A business must operate at reasonable efficiency, or it will fail to satisfy investors, workers, customers, government, or other agencies. These dissatisfactions will cause trouble of one kind or another, and planning must be done with all interests in mind. A business enterprise has no resources that it can view as "mine, with which I can do as I please."

Further, a business firm must exercise more careful control in timing transactions. It does not usually make a great difference if our personal affairs are moved back and forth in time; we often satisfy ourselves with a hamburger for lunch on weekdays so that we can enjoy filet mignon for Sunday dinner. In a business firm, time is of the essence in everything. Cooperative efforts of people cannot be allowed to vary too far from schedule, and if people appear for work, there must be materials and tools to work with; waiting costs money because it keeps facilities idle. Emphasis on time and schedules makes a firm buy things before they are needed. Materials and supplies must be bought for stock so there will be no chance of having to wait to get them. We buy services and equipment on long-term contracts to make sure we will have what we need when we want it. Disbursements are mere incidents in business affairs—the incurrence and tracing of costs is all-important. In a similar way, credit arrangements also tend to distort the significance of cash transactions as measures of day-to-day operations. If we are to make business plans in money terms, we must do more than forecast cash receipts and payments.

Managerial plans are hardly ever conceived as cash transactions. For example, there are various kinds of promotional, informative, and persuasive activities involved in making a sale; the things to be done in making delivery of product may require a number of steps, and there may be service, installation, or even educational activities required to satisfy the customer; and meanwhile, the productive operations must be continued, to meet the needs of other customers as yet unidentified. Materials bought on credit are used for operations on a day-to-day basis; workers are paid only on payday, and the amounts they get depend on withholding and other arrangements. Managerial plans cannot deal with the complicated pattern of advance and delayed payments or receipts; they must be set up in terms of resources and activities related to the operations rather than on the cash received or paid. Budgeting has to be done on an accrual basis, because this is the way that managers have to plan.

Meaning of Budgets and Budgetary Control

Now that we have reviewed the major features of managerial planning processes, we can begin to see what budgets are. Budgets are management plans that include all the expected operations and results of a future period. These plans cover all the units and divisions of the enterprise in terms of its organization structure. Budgets state formally —in terms of expected transactions—the decisions of all levels of management about the resources to be acquired, how they are to be used, and what ought to result. Budgets put the details of management plans for operations into money units, so that the results may be projected into expected financial statements. Thus, budgeting is a kind of "future tense" accounting, in which the problems of the future are met on paper before the transactions actually occur. This approach makes it possible to compare actual events with the planned ones, to establish a feedback control arrangement which makes management more systematic and more effective.

How Budget Plans Are Expressed

Individual plans of managers will be set up in mere physical units, but they will be "translated" into cost, revenue, asset, and equity figures. Budget summaries will thus produce financial reports very much like those which result from ordinary "past tense" accounting. There will be an "income" budget, or "profit plan"; this will look very much like a conventional earnings report, except that it will refer to a period in the future rather than one just closed. There will be a "position" budget, which will look very much like a balance sheet, because it will show the assets and equities that are expected to exist at the close of the budget period as a result of the transactions to be undertaken. There will be a "financial" budget or a "cash budget" that will portray the expected receipts and payments that may be expected to follow the operating transactions, to show how the various sources of funds and classes of disbursements will affect the cash or the current position. Or in some cases, the financial summary will take the form of a *pro forma* statement of funds, concerned with financing transactions, and their effects on the net working capital position. These financial summaries will be supported by departmental or divisional schedules in the same way that the ordinary accounting figures may be subclassified to match organizational responsibilities. And as a useful way to show details of acquisition of assets or services, we may have "procurement" budgets, giving information about what materials, supplies, or services we will buy, what workers we will recruit and employ, and what items of equipment or facilities we will plan to acquire.

A SUMMARY VIEW OF BUDGET PREPARATION

The process of budget preparation may be thought of as a systematic collection of managerial plans, set up at various levels and in various divisions of a business, put into relation with one another so as to make up an overall program for the firm as a whole. This is portrayed graphically in Figure 1–3.

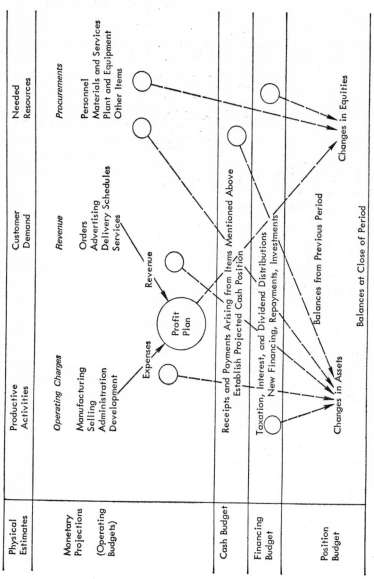

Figure 1–3. *Relations among forecasts and budget estimates*

From the basic estimating forecast (usually but not always sales volume), the expected level of operations is established. As each part of the business is viewed by its managers in terms of its share of the overall program, forecasts are made of how that section or unit will operate. For sales departments this will involve forecasts of revenue and selling costs; for other departments the forecasts will be set in terms of operating charges for each section or unit during the forthcoming period. These forecasts, combined and adjusted for inventory carry-overs, will yield estimates of expense, as well as other estimates for needed procurements of materials and supplies, personnel and services, machinery and equipment. The procurement budgets will serve to estimate necessary disbursements, while the revenue budget may be translated into expected cash receipts. These estimates will serve to point up financial needs or problems.

Matching of revenues and expenses will serve to produce a profit plan or expected earnings statement, and the effect of all these estimates upon the existing asset and equity structures will appear in a projected statement of financial position.

The net result of this process is to get the entire management staff to consider their situation and to make mutually satisfactory plans for the forthcoming periods' operations. These plans, summarized in the way we have indicated, may be tested for profitability, for financial feasibility, and for overall growth and position at the close of the period via the summary budgets. This scheme of planning has obvious advantages, and it is not hard to see why managers would find it useful. The issues of implementation and procedure involved are discussed in Chapter 2.

QUESTIONS

1. "Decision making is, in essence, forecasting and interpretation based on experience." Indicate, for a number of decision situations, the content of this statement.

2. If a decision turns out to be incorrect, is this the fault of the decision maker if the data on which he based his decision are untrustworthy?

3. Would you think the sales manager's decision to add five more salesmen to his existing staff of 50 was wrong or right under the following separate situations? Give reasons for your answers.

   (a) There were five excellent men available because a competitor had quit business. The sales manager believed the volume of sales would increase because of the competitor's decision to quit. The volume of sales did not increase.

(b) The normal attrition rate in the sales department is about 10 percent per quarter—that is, on the average, about five men quit each quarter for various reasons. Nobody quit in the ensuing quarter.

(c) The sales manager planned a special campaign to recruit new customers by calling on firms that the company had not previously served. The special campaign produced only a handful of new customers.

(d) The sales manager has, as a matter of policy, hired any and all really able men who ask for such assignments, since they are paid on commission. The commission is expected to be more than the costs of obtaining the orders, but some salesmen cannot earn enough to make their work pay. Of the five salesmen hired, only two were satisfied to remain on the job.

4. Why is analysis important in preparing data for decision making? Does feedback aid in obtaining better analysis?

5. Why should the "observation and analysis" function be delegated to an accounting system rather than to the line executive in charge of the operation?

6. Supposing that the feedback mechanism functions properly, why should there be any need for accounting reports?

7. What are the different kinds of managerial plans? How are they distinguished from one another, and why is it important to make such distinctions?

8. To what extent does the nature of a managerial plan affect its relation to organization of managerial personnel? Illustrate several different plans, indicating where these would be formulated in a typical organization. How does subject matter classification of plans aid in their function and execution?

9. What is the primary purpose of an organization chart? What other functions does it serve? Why does it sometimes fail to meet these needs?

10. Business plans tend to be expressed in money terms. Does this mean that a business budget is the same as a personal budget? Why or why not?

11. Relate the typical content of a set of financial reports (position, earnings, and fund flows) to the managerial decisions of a business enterprise. Use a flow chart to specify the relations between the plans and the financial reporting data.

12. The general ledger trial balance of the Tattersall Manufacturing Company at June 30, 19—, after all transactions and adjustments had been posted was the following:

TATTERSALL MANUFACTURING COMPANY
Trial Balance, General Ledger
June 30, 19—

Cash and bank deposits	$ 62,100	
Accounts receivable control	305,000	
Allowance, uncollectibles, etc.		$ 15,260
Materials and supplies stores control	92,000	
Work in process control	103,000	
Finished goods stock control	115,000	
Prepayments control	15,300	
Plant and equipment control	316,800	
Accumulated depreciation		87,480
Bank loans		25,000
Audited payables control		45,260
Other accrued liabilities		13,620
Sales billed (net of discounts allowed)		1,322,000
Returned sales and allowances	40,000	
Factory cost of goods shipped	996,360	
Selling cost control	116,500	
General management cost control	93,500	
Manufacturing cost control	1,062,130	
Manufacturing cost applied to product		1,060,130
Customer discounts lapsed		12,700
Purchase discounts lost	540	
Provision for uncollectibles, etc.	12,500	
Interest charges	1,200	
Taxes on income	38,200	
Capital stock (no par, 100,000 shares)		700,000
Dividends declared and paid	36,000	
Retained earnings		124,680
Totals	$3,396,130	$3,396,130

The Selling Cost Control account serves to summarize the content of 18 subsidiary ledger accounts, each covering a specific sales territory. All costs of carrying on the sales operation are detailed there, by sub-subclassifications on a natural or descriptive basis. The totals of the sub-sub columns of these ledger accounts are shown below:

Salaries and commissions	$60,600	Insurance	$700
Travel cost	21,400	Taxes on property	800
Advertising	25,100	Repairs	500
Communications (postage,		Miscellaneous (supplies, re-	
etc.)	5,900	pairs)	600
Depreciation	900		

The General Management Cost Control account is a similar summarization of the operating charges incurred by five major officials of the company (general manager, secretary, comptroller, personnel manager, and research and production engineer) and their respective staffs and subdepartments. Details, summarized from totals of sub-classifications, are the following:

Salaries and wages	$58,700	Outside professional service	$9,800
Contributions and		Depreciation of equipment	600
public relations	17,800	Insurance	500
Travel cost	2,600	Taxes on property	700
Communications	1,900	Miscellaneous (supplies, etc.)	900

The Manufacturing Cost Control account includes all the operating charges applicable to 45 factory departments engaged in the production of 15 lines of product. The details of manufacturing costs (obtained by summarizing the subclassifications in the various departmental records) are these:

Materials drawn from		Depreciation of buildings	$ 5,800
stores	$375,000	Depreciation of equipment	12,780
Wages of workmen	454,000	Depreciation of furniture	800
Salaries of other employees	175,900	Insurance expired	1,150
Supplies drawn from stores	7,600	Machinery repairs	3,200
Buildings—heat and main-		Taxes on property	5,400
tenance	12,500		
Electric light and power	8,000		

The inventories at the beginning of 19— were these:

Materials and supplies stores control	$ 85,000
Work in process control	94,230
Finished goods control	60,000
Total	$239,230

Prepare the following:

(a) Statement of Earnings in conventional form, with supporting schedule of Factory Cost of Goods Shipped.

(b) An alternative earnings statement showing *operating charges* classified in "natural" (descriptive) terms—for example, Salaries, Materials and Supplies, and so on.

(c) A position statement, set up so as to emphasize net working capital.

(d) An outline, as to content and destination, of the managerial reports that might be prepared from such a system of accounting as described here.

2

ADMINISTRATIVE ASPECTS OF BUDGET PROCEDURE

Budgeting is a way to make management more systematic. We have already stressed that decision making is in large measure dependent upon forecasts. Budget preparation is one way to get managers to plan what they propose to do in a forthcoming period, in such a way that those plans may form a consistent group of inter-related decisions. Such an approach to management problems is not only a clear recognition of the interdependence of various levels and subject areas in the planning process but also an essential part of control, and it provides a means of tying experience with planning to ensure that operations are carried on as they should be.

It has been suggested that business decisions are numerous and complex and that the overall task of decision making must be divided over a number of managers in the interest of using skills, experience, and judgment in the most effective ways. Yet the decisions made by those managers must be put together into a balanced and coherent plan for the company as a whole. This is a difficult task, and we thus need to consider what administrative approaches must be built into the budget program. We shall be concerned with who should make forecasts and estimates, how the various plans may be kept in line with divisional strategies or company policy, and what review and revision may be needed to make individual plans compatible and consistent with one another. In short, we will survey the relations that must be established within the structure to which budgeting is applied.

NEED FOR SOME CENTRALIZED CONTROL

One part of budget preparation must be centralized. The task of putting the estimates and plans together into the desired "financial report" patterns is not one that can be divided among many people. There ought to be some focal point through which all the various kinds of financial and statistical data may flow; where questions of procedure, methods of analysis, or interpretation may be raised; and where tentative proposals may be reviewed for completeness, consistency, and compatibility with other plans. This point is usually set up in a company by designating some official as budget officer, financial planner, or other similar title. The nature of this officer's responsibility suggests that he should be closely associated with the chief financial officer—the controller, treasurer, or vice-president, finance. Typically, the budget function (that is, the review and facilitation of budgetary processes) is assigned to an assistant controller in a large company or to the controller in a small one. This is logical because of the close relation that ought to exist between the planning of financial events and the measurement of them as they actually occur. While the budget officer does not make the plans, he does put them together in summary terms, and he uses the accounting system to provide the feedback that is necessary for managers to check their performance. Integration of the budget system is thus furthered by the use of staff personnel in the accounting department to analyze and report on the budget system.

Relation between Line and Staff Functions

There are important distinctions between the "line" and the "staff" functions within an enterprise. Managers that are concerned with major and essential operations of the business—such as sales, production, customer service, construction, and the like—are termed "line" or operating managers. Managers who render service to line managers in the way of purchasing, personnel, or maintenance functions, who provide information through accounting or statistical activities, or who offer advice in the form of engineering or market analysis are "staff" people. Staff officers such as financial planners and accountants should not have any direct part in the making of operating decisions which are the prerogative of line officers. Staff officers are expected to provide information or advice, to help line managers do their work better; but decisions about the line operations and the consequences of those decisions must remain with those to whom the primary responsibility has been assigned.

This is also true of such staff functions as purchasing, personnel, and public relations. Sometimes these can be very important parts of the management machine; if purchasing is of grave significance in the fortunes of the firm, the purchasing executive may be a vice-president, even though he may still be a staff officer. But no purchasing agent (vice-president or not) would presume to tell a production official—especially one at lower rank—what kind of material he should use for a given part or product. He might make strong recommendations to the chief production executive for changes in materials specifications or in sources of supply—he might even go so far as to make suggestions about possible materials whose use could reduce costs or increase quality of output, even though they might require some alterations in the production methods. But the decision on materials specifications and the methods of production would have to be left with the production manager—otherwise he cannot be held responsible for results. Staff people must "stay out of the way" of line decisions, for their own and the company's best interests.

STAFF ACTIVITIES WITHIN LINE DEPARTMENTS—SALES. There may be staff functions at any level of organization, even within line management areas. In Figure 2–1, market research, advertising, and sales promotion are staff functions for the assistants of the sales vice-president. These people have the same relation to the vice-president, sales as the financial vice-president has to the president, general manager. The mere name applied to a function does not, however, settle whether it is line or staff. For instance, the function labeled "foreign offices" might be a line function, in that the head of that operation might be in direct control of sales offices in a number of foreign countries, with complete authority over those activities. Or the foreign office function might be a group concerned with making economic studies of foreign markets to guide the vice-president, sales and the foreign sales chief in planning and control of such activities. In this case, since there is no other assignment in foreign marketing, it is perhaps easier to assume that the foreign office's function is a line operation. The test of such an interpretation is, of course, the nature of the control that the manager in question may exercise. Tasks may be assigned in many ways, and the organization chart is not always the way to distinguish among the various arrangements.

LINE ACTIVITIES IN STAFF DEPARTMENTS—FINANCE. Figure 2–2 shows a typical arrangement of functions within the purview of the financial vice-president of a moderately large company. Here there are line functions within the staff area; since the unit of operations is here the finance function, the conception of line shifts to another pattern. In this grouping, the "tax and legal" function may be the only staff operation from the financial vice-president's viewpoint. "Tax and

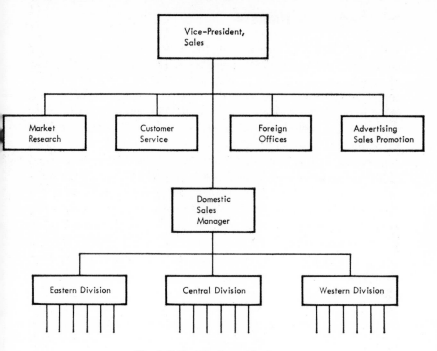

Figure 2–1. *Typical organization of a sales division*

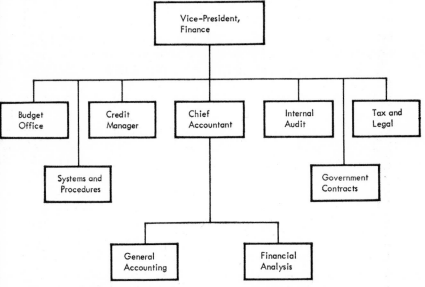

Figure 2–2. *Typical organization of a finance division*

legal" may have the job of keeping the rest of the finance department informed of the import of legal and tax matters upon operations, and he may be concerned with helping people decide about *how* certain contracts and transactions should be handled to avoid difficulties and costs. In one sense, staff officers are a little like consultants who come to the firm to study problems and make reports and recommendations based on their specialized abilities and viewpoints; they are valued helpers, but they do not "run" the business. The budget officer may cause real problems and create much confusion if he fails to recognize the limits on his (and other people's) authority to make operating decisions. His task is to inform, to give advice or suggestions, to help or encourage those who have responsibility for operations, but otherwise to stay out of the way.

The budget officer has another important function—to precipitate, request, and press for operating decisions *to be made* by those who should make them. That is, issues that ought to be settled may have to be called to a line officer's attention when decisions are necessary. In many cases, one of the most useful contributions of a staff officer is to press for decisions that are needed. The notion of feedback control requires decisions when operations do not conform to plan. Merely reporting the condition does not correct anything; it may be necessary to apply pressure in appropriate ways so that the needed adjustments will be promptly made. This may be a central element in the budget officer's job—he often serves as the catalyst to precipitate managers' decisions.

HOW BUDGETS ARE INITIATED

The budget officer does not make up the budget, even though he may be the one most interested in the success of the budget plan. The reason for this is that those who must live with the operating plans and take responsibility for their execution should have a large say in deciding what those plans should be. People readily accept orders when the issues involved are not crucially important to themselves or when they are willing to yield to what they regard as better informed judgment. But it is not hard to see why a person likes to have a part in making the plans he is expected to carry out or in setting the standards by which his success will be judged.

Even more important, however, is the fact that only those who have participated in making plans can be held completely responsible for carrying them out. One who is doing what he himself planned to do cannot very well shift the blame for results; performance that does not match the plan can arise from only two sources—poor planning or inadequate "follow-through"—and either way, he is accountable. "Passing the buck" may thus be reduced. Therefore, budget estimates should be initiated as far down in the organization structure as possible—as close as they can be to the level at which the work is carried on. By this approach, operating problems and issues can be faced four-square; issues can be brought into the open for examination and discussion, and they can be settled where they arise. The decision process may thus proceed upward from the level of day-to-day operations to the levels of strategy and policy, allowing for review and adjustment whenever problems appear. But the decision process should move up and down the organization structure. Although operating plans should originate near the bottom of the organization chart and flow upward as they are integrated into more general forms, there should also be a downward communication, because operations must fit into the overall aims of the company as a whole. Company aims are seldom visible at the operating levels; the punch-press department foreman probably has little interest in the reasons for limiting the geographical expansion of sales territories or in what this may have to do with the number and kinds of parts to be made. However, the foreman must be told about company aims and plans which may affect him. Otherwise, his plans will be inadequate or inconsistent with overall company planning.

The Budget Letter

The need for an understanding of company position and aims is frequently met by starting the budget process with a general letter from the chairman or president of the company to his subordinates. This letter is based upon a thorough review of the outlook for the national economy and the industry, political developments and situations, social trends and activities, all in their relation to company objectives and policies. The letter may indicate that as a result of this review, the chief executive believes that this is the time to expand, to develop new products, to add channels of distribution, or to proceed into expansion or diversification programs. Or, under other circumstances, the letter may point out the need for retrenchment, more cautious husbanding of resources, less vigorous pursuit of new ways to expand operations. The purpose of the letter is to set the tone and the general scope of the company program; these ideas may be discussed, reworked, or made more specific at the top management level, through an executive committee or a budget and finance committee, in which major officials (top-level line and staff managers) work together to validate or clarify the general proposals. Then these proposals are distributed to the lower organization levels, becoming more detailed and specific at each step. This flow of information and discussion serves to relate the overall company viewpoint to the operations of various divisions, departments, and other units. Each manager thus starts his own planning with an idea of the overall program of which his plan will be a part. This promotes understanding and cooperation. When the detailed plans prepared at lower levels of management are passed upward for review and assimilation, they are more likely to fit together without conflict. This approach alerts the entire management group to produce the kind of teamwork that makes the enterprise really effective.

Data for Planning

Another way to see how budgets are initiated is to look at the sources of data that are used in planning. One cannot plan well without some basis for his expectations. Managers use their knowledge and experience to make their plans realistic and meaningful. Much of this background is informal; it may be quite general, and it is sometimes incomplete, perhaps only partly understood. But business operations depend on this background even when it is only "judgment." Perhaps the best—and often the only—way to find out what is really important in planning and controlling an operation is to ask the man who runs it.

Management background and experience are vital to planning. But the kinds of information that are needed are varied, and there is nearly always good reason to want more detailed data than a typical manager will have at his fingertips. He must have some kind of records to keep track of data he will need for his work.

Accounting reports are helpful to management in this regard; they show the results of the operations in objective financial terms, and they indicate the effects of decisions that have been made. By knowing what *has* happened, one can better see what will happen under similar conditions. Every manager—foreman, section chief, or vice-president—should know what it costs to run the operations for which he is responsible. Each sales representative or supervisor up to the vice-president, sales ought to know what sales have been made in his bailiwick—expressed in both dollars and in physical units. Cost and

Figure 2–3

CONVENTIONAL MANUFACTURING COMPANY
Departmental Cost Report Form
18th period, 19——, May 5, 19——, Department 26

	Controllable Costs										Uncontrollable Costs			
	Di-rect Labor	In-direct Labor	Over-time	Fringe Labor Costs	Di-rect Ma-terials	Sup-plies	Power	Tools	Re-pairs	Super-vision, Office	Other	Depre-ciation, Amor-tization	Build-ing Space	Gen. Admin. Over-head	Other
This period															
Budget															
Over or (under)															
Year to date															
Budget															
Over or (under)															
Last year, this period															
Budget															
Over or under															

revenue data should be tabulated and reported promptly and at reasonably short intervals. Stale information is not useful, and too large a collection of data over too long a period is hard to interpret for planning purposes. It is important that cause and effect relationships be observed and that changing conditions be easily followed. Cost and revenue data should be compared with budget and with the results in past periods—last month or last year—for these comparisons often suggest reasons or conditions that are not otherwise apparent. The report form should also provide for feedback of explanatory information to the manager's boss, who should receive similar reports covering all the units in his jurisdiction. A typical department cost report appears in Figure 2–3.

Reports of this kind will carry the amount of detail that is important for the managers who receive them. Those reports covering operations at lower levels of the organization will show the most detail. Reports for managers with broader responsibilities will show less detail, being summaries of those made up for his subordinates. Often, a middle or top manager will receive copies of reports made to his immediate subordinates.

Reports to management are often supplemented by statistical or other analyses, such as classification of costs (or sales) by product or parts groups or other useful arrangements. There may be seasonal or trend analyses, or studies of different kinds of variance in cost or sales patterns. The reports should give each manager a clear picture of the results for which he is responsible and as much other information as can be used effectively in controlling operations. The data on these reports will be used to make up budget plans, as well as to follow the way in which those plans compare with actual results. This aspect of budget preparation is another reason why there should be a budget officer in the finance and accounting division to serve as liaison with management in matters of budgetary control.

APPROACHES TO FORECASTING

There are a number of ways in which past data may be used in planning future operations, each more or less useful in particular circumstances. We could plan by merely assuming a continuation or extension of past experience, or we might try to improve on the past by using those data in a more sophisticated and effective way.

Extension of Past Operations

The president's budget letter might suggest that the forthcoming budget period would be only slightly different from the preceding one. In this case, one might be tempted to follow this notion literally and plan for an exact repetition of past activities. Indeed, sometimes this is as good as can be done. It has the merit of starting from an actually accomplished pattern, and there cannot be much doubt of being able to do exactly what was done before.

The trouble with such an approach is that it assumes that past operations were satisfactory—that we ought to be satisfied to do the same thing over again. But this is not really a safe assumption. Whatever inadequacies or inefficiencies existed in the past will be accepted and repeated in the future. This seems to deny that we can learn by experience. There ought always to be some chance for improvement in any activity—at least we should never cease looking for it. To accept the past as a blueprint for the future denies the possibility of progress.

But extension of the past has other weaknesses. Changing conditions may entail adjustments of various kinds, even though from the viewpoint expressed in the president's letter, they do not appear to be important. The relative importance of different operations may change; the perpetuation of these arrangements maintains the relationships that exist, even when certain functions or activities become unnecessary or useless. One of the great evils of bureaucracy is the perpetuation of good works long after they are needed or wanted, regardless of future trends or needs.

This is particularly true with respect to coordination or balancing of activities. Extending past performance is not a good way to budget unless there is no chance for improvement in departmental relations and no change in any of the related programs. That is, product design, market penetration, methods of sale, production, or other operations—all the various aspects of the enterprise would have to remain unchanged for a budget based on extended past experience to be of use.

Rigid Rate of Change Patterns

There are situations (notably common in government and eleemosynary institutions) in which budgeting is attempted on a "flat percentage increase" pattern. That is, last year's budget is simply recast at a uniformly higher level. If this does reflect any management planning, it is obviously not the result of much analysis. Any attempt to increase or decrease the rate of activity (or cost or revenue) for the enterprise is bound to involve some choices as to how the increase or reduction should affect operating units of various kinds. Some activities perhaps ought to be increased while others are declining. In the company with declining sales, efforts devoted to product and market research and improvement in technical processes probably should be increased rather than decreased when revenues fall off.

There are many ties among the various administrative units of an enterprise. Some of these are obvious and have been suggested in the preceding chapter. What is produced by the manufacturing division must be acceptable to the sales division as meeting customer wants. Productive operations give rise to procurement needs for personnel, services, supplies, materials, or equipment. All of these activities raise questions which concern finance and various maintenance and other service facilities.

But there are still other inter-relations. Not only are there many occasions for intercommunication and joint decisions which do not clearly appear in the organization chart, but activities such as inspection or scheduling involve mutual adjustments between departments or sections. A change of method in one section may solve a quality control problem in a subsequent process. Overtime in one department may avoid idle time in another; idle time may exist even while customers are clamoring for delivery. Within a given managerial jurisdiction, there is no reason to assume that patterns are fixed—cost-wise or in any other way. A change in price, quality, or even the method of shipment of incoming materials may entail changes in other materials costs, in labor, power, supplies, repairs, or other items. A late receipt of certain strategic supplies may alter production schedules, putting critical orders aside and making fill-ins of other work necessary, despite the obvious need to work overtime at a later date.

Standards and Other Building Blocks

The situation just described means that the planning of operations cannot be attempted without some recognition of these internal relationships. Thus, in every firm—even when there is no attempt to budget in a formal way—there are a large number of elementary relations that must be understood by managers. Many of these are embodied in the background information developed by experience and used as "rules of thumb." But others may be established in other ways: the speed, feed, and other specifications for operating a machine; the characteristics of certain materials and the ways in which they may be used (for example, the use of bar stock to make parts of certain specifications by merely sawing to length rather than turning parts on a lathe). In addition, there are relations between certain items of operating procedure and the costs incurred; these will occupy our attention in more detail when we consider cost behavior in Chapter 3. The point in all this is that these various elements in operating procedures can be combined and controlled in a wide variety of ways. The attempt to set up a satisfactory plan of operations should be based on this kind of analytical understanding, rather than a mere extension or adjustment of past-period experience.

The Basic Estimating Factor

There is a need to centralize the planning of the various parts of the enterprise, and there are also advantages to be gained by adjusting various internal plans to optimum balance by the use of internal standards and relationships. To do this, a basic factor is necessary that can serve as the overall or central forecasting basis, to which all the operating budgets will be related. For many companies, the basic estimating factor is sales, expressed in physical units as well as in terms of dollar revenue to be expected. The use of sales forecasts as a central theme on which to base the budget structure has certain advantages.

The basic estimating factor should be one that represents the central target of operating decisions, so as to provide the backbone of the entire budget program. But it also needs to be something which ties the firm as a unit to its general environment. Every business has some critical contact with the economy as a whole, where managerial control and decision making involve adjustment of the firm to its environment. This contact or connection is the place where management must deal with uncontrollable factors, such as the market for its product, the source of materials or labor, and the nature and extent of governmental, geographical, or financial restraints in activities of the enterprise. This is where the enterprise and its management must acclimate itself to things outside their own sphere of operations.

For most companies, the point of adjustment to its environment is sales. Although we may try to impress or influence the customer with our products and services, we cannot escape the fact that the customer does have the last word on whether or not he will buy. The market is where our efforts are judged, and customers determine what we must do to win their approval in sales. Therefore, the sales forecast is usually the first step in budgeting, and it is the basic estimate to which the rest of the budget program is geared.

But sometimes sales do not represent the limiting factor in enterprise operations, and budgeting must start from some other basic forecast. A public utility, for instance, does not deal with sales in a promotional sense. Even though the company may do something toward increasing the use made of its services, the effect cannot be very great. There is no substitute or direct competition in the market, and customer response by way of purchase decisions is very limited, for the customer does not have much choice to express. There are not many variations in electric currents, water, or gas supply. The volume of business done by a utility company really depends more on population, standards of living, or climate than it does on anything the company can offer. Further, the amount of service the utility can make available is limited by its plant. Fluctuations in the volume of business cannot be adjusted or met by the production of stock items to be stored in inventory. The public utility company is more concerned with meeting maximum demands for service than it is with customers' market choices. It will tend to budget in terms of using its plant most effectively to meet daily or weekly fluctuations in customer demand rather than working very hard to influence sales as such.

Resource Scarcity

There are situations in which sales may be of much less importance for management planning than the availability of needed resources. For example, there may be only a certain number of properly trained workers available. Even though the demand for a company's product may be very large, the volume of operations could be limited by the lack of worker skills. This, of course, could be overcome in time—workers might be hired away from other employers, or additional workers may be trained or imported from other places. Sometimes these things are not possible within the constraints of time and condition. For example, a mine located in a wilderness area may have its volume of operations limited by the number of workers available.

Under some conditions the supply of materials may be the limiting factor in projecting company activities. In times of scarcity, the shortage of materials may force a company to find substitutes, reduce the volume of operations, even convert to some other business, or shut down entirely. Even in normal conditions there are cases in which the materials supply dictates the level of operations and represents the factor to which management must adjust.

Finances may also be a limiting factor on the volume of business, as in some government or eleemosynary operations. Management cannot always decide how much service should be made available when there is no way to tell whether it is wanted or will be used. Under these conditions the amount of funds available will sometimes be the basis for planning general activities such as research and information services.

The use of some factor to forecast the level of operations does not preclude there being other restrictions on other aspects of managerial choice. The enterprise will use as a basic estimating factor whatever appears to be the central or most important condition to which the enterprise must conform. Using the sales estimate as the basic forecast suggests that sales are a major restraint on company operations; and this in turn implies that it is more effective to orient the forecasting process around the sales program rather than otherwise.

FORECASTING THE BASIC ESTIMATING FACTOR

The attempt to forecast the basic estimating factor is an important part of budget procedure. If all the company plans are to be oriented to the expected sales, it is important that the forecast should be carefully made. We ought to take special pains to see that the whole program is not warped and jeopardized by an inadequate and untrustworthy sales forecast.

Sales are not easy to forecast. Some products have highly volatile demand characteristics, and to bring a forecast to any reasonable level of dependability may be very difficult. Indeed, it may sometimes appear to be not worth the effort, and budget programs can fail when this view is accepted. A dependable forecast is, of course, desirable; but the fact that we try to forecast at all is a long step toward understanding the sales market. Even if we can allow for only a few factors that will influence sales, we are better able to cope with the problem. Observing the errors in the crude stage of forecasting will give clues that will help establish other things to consider in the next forecast. Having even a simple idea of how far wrong a forecast may be at least sets some bench marks for adjustment. We may thus be better prepared to make those adjustments in payroll, materials acquisitions, and so on when they may be necessary.

But most important, it must be recognized that the strongest reason for attempting to forecast is that we cannot avoid it. When we make any decision—rational or otherwise—we act as if we knew the future. Every decision—to hire workers, acquire materials, repair equipment, or anything else—implies that we know the need for these services and how the resulting product will be disposed of. We either actually do know these things, or we must act just as if we did. To make decisions requires that we do the best we can in forecasting, because we cannot avoid following through and accepting responsibility.

There are a number of ways to approach the problem of forecasting as applied to budgeting. Some of these are explained briefly below —not as technical procedures to be mastered, but as useful tools for forecasting business events.

Share of Market Approach

Sales forecasts can be based on the premise that a determinable part of the national income is allocable to the sales of a given industry and that the single company's share of that industry's sales can be stated with confidence. There are a number of predictions of Gross National Product or National Income made every year by recognized authorities. Granted that the sales of the industry and the company share can be specified, the sales forecast is easy to make. Strategic plans of the company can be oriented to changes in the market share; the changes in market share are thus fairly precise short-run goals for the company. The market share approach to a sales forecast is likely to be very useful in connection with staple products and well-ordered industry patterns of competition.

Trend and Cycle Projections

Starting with the trend of sales established over a period of years, a forecast of future sales may be made by extending this trend, but making some allowance for the effects of cyclical factors. If the sales trend for the company has been an increase of 5 percent per year, but the cycle prediction is for a decline in business activity of 10 percent during the forthcoming year, it would be reasonable to take the trend and cycle figures into account, setting next year's sales at 94.5 percent of last year's results. This estimate is somewhat rough, but it has the merit of recognizing essential patterns in the growth and operating history of the firm or the industry. Tempered with some judgment, trend and cycle analysis may be of considerable usefulness in forecasting sales.

Field Surveys

One common approach to sales forecasting is the field survey. Sometimes this is set up as a research investigation to establish the reasons for consumer preferences, the existence of buying habits, or other market factors. But it is also possible to conduct surveys that throw light on market shares, trends, changes in demand, or even to project sales that should be expected from given market areas and under given conditions. Surveys are often conducted by outside agencies on a consulting basis, but they also may be designed and carried out by company personnel.

We have already suggested that the best way to find out about an operation is to ask the man who runs it. This can be applied to sales forecasting. Sales people know their product, their market, and their customers. Hence, their predictions of future sales are likely to be more valid for this reason. At least, they have closer contact with the situation than one who must depend upon industry statistics or outside consultants for his data. Further, the salesman who has predicted his own sales may try a bit harder to justify his judgment, especially if he really believes he knows his job. Of course, it may be advantageous to underestimate sales if one is to be held accountable for fulfilling the estimate. But this is not hard to detect, because other data may be used to test the reasonableness of self-set quotas.

One advantage in a survey approach is that the estimates tend to be made in such a way as to yield data on expectations with regard to particular products and territories. Data classified in this way are more useful for projecting production output by products and give some indication of shifts in the territorial sectors of the market. These projections may have much to do with company plans for warehousing or branch plant operations.

Sometimes the sales survey approach is modified by having the regional or district managers set sales quotas on the basis of statistical data or their own judgment, but letting the salesmen discuss these allotments, indicating why they consider them too low or too high. This kind of interaction is stimulating, and it can produce more seasoned expectations. If there are "product managers" as well as territorial sales jurisdictions, an even more spirited approach and analysis may be precipitated.

The survey approach is sometimes thought to be of limited usefulness, since sales personnel are believed to be overoptimistic or overpessimistic as their situation changes. But it is hard to believe that people who work with customers and sales situations all the time cannot know their market and their problems better than outsiders.

Regression Analysis

Theoretically, the best way to relate sales to underlying but independent variables is by statistical regression analysis. From a scientific viewpoint, the inter-relation of forces may be analyzed by measuring their association in quantitative terms and writing an equation from which sales (the dependent variable) are estimated from other statistical observations of relationship (regression coefficients). The logic of this approach may be illustrated by the obvious relation between the sale of building materials and other variables that condition the demand for housing—such as birth and marriage data, immigration, formation and relocation of certain industrial complexes, levels of employment, and disposable income. If data such as these are analyzed carefully, it is possible to develop some guidance from even the most complex situation. If certain lags and leads in the fluctuations can be established, the expected validity in the forecast may be even more enhanced.

Combinations of Method

It has already been hinted that a reason for using more than one forecasting method is that they can check on each other. Thus, it is not uncommon for the budget officer to inject comments or information about alternative forecasts into a sales budget conference. Such action serves to raise issues that may need to be discussed. Even though this may have the effect of basing the forecast on compromise as well as impersonal analysis, it also tends to avoid heavy bias or logical errors in the sales forecast. A sales estimate that cannot stand comparison with alternative methods is not likely to be a safe basis for budget planning; one that represents a compromise which appears reasonable to the various managerial viewpoints involved contributes even more to the group effort by enlisting cooperative action among those whose views must be unified.

Forecasting Selling Costs

The forecast of sales is based on some set of operations and related costs of carrying on the sales effort. This may be assumed to be the same as was done in the period just closed, but any attempt to forecast sales must raise the question of whether or not the selling cost pattern will be changed. The volume of sales can sometimes be increased if added promotional expenditures are possible, if a larger sales staff may be recruited, or if efforts are made to call upon customers and cultivate territorial areas more intensively. The question of how much to spend and how to spend it ought, of course, to be decided by the sales executives, and this raises some difficult problems. It is not always easy to see how much of an effect may be expected from added outlays for sales promotion efforts; the relations between expenditures and results are not too well-defined. This is probably because the underlying causes are psychological rather than physical, and there may be time lags and joint effects involved. We can seldom be certain that the sales of one product do not affect the sales of other products, or that the reactions of customers to various sales appeals will follow any precisely determinable pattern. But here, as in other budgeting situations, any decision at all implies that we have at least guessed at what effects the action will have. And if we observe and try to understand our forecasting errors, we may get a better view of what lies behind them.

Timing of Sales Projections

Most companies tie the budget preparation to a sales forecast (and the accompanying selling cost projections). This means that the sales budget must be at least fairly well settled before any other budget plans can be established. Therefore, at least a tentative sales program is put together in a fairly short time after the president's letter is released. As we shall see, there will be opportunities to revise or adjust the sales forecast after other phases of the profit plan have been drawn up. But the preliminary sales estimates are needed at the beginning of the planning period to make a start possible.

This immediately suggests that one of the ways to deal with the problem of sales forecasting is to keep working at it, making some rough sales forecasts in the ordinary course of operations, even when there is no pressure for preparing a formal sales budget. Most sales departments do something of this kind, through a more or less continuous attempt to follow current developments in the market and to predict sales for the immediate future in the form of quotas or other expectations. Occasionally, these short-term (weekly or monthly) expectations are expanded to cover somewhat longer periods. The sales department is, therefore, in a good position to meet requests for projected sales plans. The very nature of the sales operation tends to emphasize future prospects, and it generally creates a forward looking viewpoint in those people who work at sales jobs.

Detail in Sales Estimates

We have discussed sales estimates up to this point as if all that was needed was a dollar revenue figure, or at least a mere overall and summary total of the sales plan in some one kind of physical volume. This is a bit unrealistic. Most companies have more than one item in the product line, or at least a number of styles, sizes, or other variations. The "mix" of products is important, not only because these products have different effects on sales, but because the variety of products must be known or guessed at to plan production operations.

Sometimes the product makeup in the sales program can be kept in mind all the way through the sales forecasting by making all sales estimates in terms of specific products. It is also possible to have a general sales forecast subdivided into product lines by setting separate figures through each product division, if the firm is organized that way. Sometimes, however, the product mix is not taken into account in the initial sales estimates but is established by allocation or averaging the overall level of sales in dollars or tonnage. This could be useful when the various products differ only slightly. But sometimes this must be estimated when competition forces producers to vary their product according to minor preferences of customers. Forecasting auto sales in terms of number of vehicles is not too difficult, but it is almost impossible to guess what customers will actually order in choosing from a large number of combinations of engines, transmissions, body styles, color and trim options, and numerous built-in or added accessories. The only way to plan production in such a case is to build the various components to individual standards, so they can be combined as needed. Guessing at the probable range of choices makes possible some tentative scheduling of production of these components, subject to change if the guesses turn out to be wrong.

The use of experience averages is, in cases like these, justified by the fact that general preferences (one type of engine or transmission as compared to others) usually change only slowly over time. But this needs to be watched, for when an abrupt change does appear, quick adjustment is needed. This is the reason that some companies find it necessary to keep production schedules flexible, setting the rate of output and the mix of products only for short periods, such as a week or a month at a time.

This may be of even greater importance when sales vary in a seasonal pattern, which must be taken into account. Usually it is easier (and safer) to forecast for a short period than for a long one, and the sales forecast may be made in two parts. The first part projects a detailed volume and revenue for, say, the first quarter of the year by months; the other forecast is for the total sales over the other nine months of the year. This gives a specific set of goals for the short view and a general one over the longer period. Sometimes this pattern is followed on a continuing basis. For example, at the end of the second month, one might project the second quarter in detail and extend the estimated nine months' total to cover the first quarter of the next year. Thus, the pattern of forecasting keeps moving ahead of operations—three months in detail and nine months more in single total. Managers are thus informed not only of immediate prospects and how these (seasonal as well as others) fluctuations will affect operations, but also are kept aware of the longer-period pattern, which emphasizes trend and cycle fluctuations.

Projections of sales as the basic estimating factor puts the process of forecasting on a positive basis. Plans are made in terms of expectations that are concrete and closely related to operating decisions in manufacturing, procurement, service, and other divisions of the company. When sales are forecasted, we have a grip on the whole system of estimates that will enter the budget program.

SUMMARY

In this chapter we have discussed the process of budget preparation to develop the following ideas. Budgets are one form of overall management operation, not a mere technical activity. Thus, the administration of budgeting is an operation that follows the organization plan of the company so far as decision making is concerned. Budgeting is, however, a kind of operation that can make use of specialized staff assistance, and usually the job of establishing the ways in which budget forecasts will be handled is assigned to a budget officer in the financial and accounting department of the firm. This officer has the task of facilitating, implementing, and promoting the budget program, and in addition to combining various estimates and forecasts and making reviews or analyses of such proposals, he (or his assistants) will have the responsibility for using budgets to interpret the actual operating results as tabulated by the accounting system.

The form of reporting and analysis will, of course, be different in different companies, but the principles are clear. Each operating manager should have a voice in formulating his own plans and in reviewing reports of his operations. These reports should separate controllable items (payroll costs, materials, supplies, and the like) from uncontrollable ones (depreciation, space charges, overhead allocations). Operating budgets ought to be tied to those reports, so that each manager can see how the actual operating data compare with his forecasts. There should also be other comparisons where these are useful.

Each supervisor should receive copies of the reports given to those who report to him; the actual results ought to be discussed, interpreted, and replanned in collaboration, just as the original plans and forecasts were discussed when they were made. Such a procedure tends to keep operating activities more closely in line with policies and strategy decisions at higher levels. This program, followed throughout the organization, serves to promote an entire system of responsibility accounting, in which management decisions and their results are prepared and studied by those who produce them.

We have indicated some of the ways in which forecasts may be prepared. But underlying any system of budgeting must be some basic estimating factor that is related to the president's budget letter and that has real influence on all the operations that must be planned. Typically, this basic estimating factor is sales; this may be set up in only broad outline as dollar revenue, or it may be detailed to show physical units of various products to be sold in different territories or to various kinds of customers. The more detailed the basic estimate, the simpler will be the rest of budget planning. Yet there are situations which limit the possibility of detailed sales forecasts. Each management must understand its own problems and deal with them as best it can.

Forecasting is not merely deciding to continue what has been done in the past; usually it is necessary to adjust or project the effects of changes. This makes careful analysis important, and the attempt to forecast share of market or trend and cycle must depend upon statistical regression analysis or field surveys of one kind or another. Often a combination of methods is a good way to avoid the errors and combine the advantages of different approaches.

QUESTIONS

1. "There is a clear parallel between the preparation and the enforcement of budgets and the handling of everyday decisions. Although there is of necessity some centralized control, the entire process of budgeting is one in which many people exercise various functions for the benefit of the firm as a whole." Discuss this statement, in terms of an example or illustration.

2. Of what significance is the distinction between line and staff functions, especially as related to accounting and budgetary control? Give examples of what would happen when advice is allowed to become decision making.

3. Why doesn't the president or the budget officer make up the budget? Aren't these two people in a better position to visualize the overall issues and the problems to be met?

4. If the president does not actively prepare the budget, of what use is the president's letter?

5. What does the accounting system contribute to the planning aspects of budgeting?

6. What is meant by a "controllable cost"—(a) one which is completely under the jurisdiction of a given manager, (b) one which the manager can control in even the slightest degree, or (c) some combination of the two? How would you suggest this definition could be established in the particular case of, say, social security taxes, electric power and light, or storeroom services?

7. Why should middle or top managers receive reports with less detail if they also receive copies of those reports sent to their subordinates?

8. "The future is always an extension of the past—we cannot understand that which we have not in some way experienced; and if we always build on the sound foundation of what we know from past experience, we cannot ever be very far wrong." Is this statement correct or not? Why?

9. Research and development are problem children of budgeting because they cannot be related to anything else in the financial picture. When it is feasible to make such expenditures, they are less needed; when they are really needed, there's no basis for carrying them out. How do you solve this problem?

10. What is a "basic estimating factor"? How can it be different things— sales, purchases, labor supply, and so on—in different companies? Could it be different for a given company in two successive years? Explain.

11. The following data are available concerning the operations of Mallet Company, a subsidiary of Hammer Corporation. Mallet operates in an East Asian country.

Year	Variable x (Millions)	Sales This Industry (Millions)	Sales This Company (Millions)
1	$82,617	$10,000	$1,000
2	73,303	9,010	870
3	61,966	7,796	730
4	47,367	5,542	503 *
5	46,273	5,306	511
6	52,865	6,297	531
7	58,493	7,011	748 †
8	67,957	8,116	829
9	72,275	8,903	897
10	66,117	8,321	903 ‡
11	70,601	8,543	942
12	76,220	8,996	1,109
13	91,910	11,085	1,152 §

* Price reductions.
† Quality of product improved.
‡ New dealer policies, sales force increased.
§ Introduction of TV advertising.

The following data are available to the budget officer of the Mallet Company. Variable x is predicted to reach a level of 95,220 for year 14; the sales budget for the company has already been set at $1,545, but not yet approved by top management.

(a) Would you accept the sales budget without qualification?

(b) What supplementary analysis would you want to see to check the validity of the relation of variable x to your problem?

(c) What limitations are there to the use of such an estimate as the relations between variable x and the sales of the Mallet Company?

12. The monthly sales of a given product are as follows:

	Year 1	Year 2	Year 3
January	$ 200,000	$ 220,000	$ 240,000
February	240,000	256,000	272,000
March	250,000	270,000	284,000
April	280,000	310,000	320,000
May	320,000	350,000	374,000
June	320,000	340,000	370,000
July	330,000	364,000	400,000
August	340,000	382,000	420,000
September	300,000	304,000	320,000
October	260,000	266,000	280,000
November	240,000	250,000	264,000
December	200,000	224,000	230,000
Total	$3,280,000	$3,536,000	$3,774,000

(a) Compute the monthly percentage of annual sales for each month; compare these, and calculate the average for each month over the three year period.

(b) Plot these monthly averages cumulatively to show the average cumulation of sales by months over the year.

(c) The year 4 forecast of sales was $4,150,000. The first three months' results in year 4 are January, $280,600; February, $336,000; and March, $351,600. How, if at all, would you suggest the year 4 forecast be adjusted at the end of March?

3

TECHNICAL FACTORS IN BUDGET PLANS

Up to this point, we have been primarily concerned with the underlying management notions related to budget planning and control. We have set up some general conceptions of the nature of budgets and the administrative procedures which make the budget officer and various operating managers work together as a team, each contributing his part to the overall plan of operations for the firm as a whole. We have seen the start of budget preparation in the use of the president's budget letter and in the approaches to forecasting sales.

Now we are ready to apply technical factors in the planning process, so that plans of operation may be expressed in financial terms. To do this, we shall consider the way in which the length of the budget period may be established, how production estimates may be expressed as parts and assembly requirements, what inventory policy has to do with budget plans, and how operating costs behave in relation to volume of operations or input factors. This will provide bases for departmental cost schedules, procurement budgets, and other plans.

THE LENGTH OF THE BUDGET PERIOD

This issue has already received some attention under the heading of sales forecasting. It was pointed out that a short period makes forecasting easier, in the sense that fewer distorting influences can enter the forecasting problem. On the other hand, a forecast based on an extremely short period does not give very much of a basis for extended planning. It does not raise very significant questions, and questions are the things that precipitate decision making.

There are no precise limits to the horizons that may be set in planning. Long-range forecasts may cover periods as long as 20 years or more; the need for the dial system in telephone communication was established fully 30 years before the system was initiated. Many research and development plans recognize ten-year to 15-year horizons; television was experimentally accomplished in the late 1920s but marketed in 1950. Capital budgeting decisions in the typical business firm must consider at least the economic life span of the equipment under review, typically five to 20 years. Some companies attempt to forecast the general levels of operation (sales, plant expenditures, and long-term financing) for at least five years, and public utilities do this for much longer periods. Automobile designs are typically frozen two to three years before production is started. One-year budget forecasts in this context appear to be quite short.

The One-Year Period

Conventional notions have something to do with the selection of an accounting or budgeting period. The idea of a twelve-month year as a fundamental time unit is quite firmly entrenched—perhaps there is some justification for this in the fact that seasonal patterns are repetitive. Aside from this, however, there is no obvious reason why a period of 365¼ days should be preferred to some longer or shorter one. Since forecasts and plans are less likely to be accurate over a year than over shorter periods, there is good reason to prefer a semiannum or a quarter. Yet as the planning period is shortened, "averaging out" tends to be reduced, and minor factors begin to show up. For example, if we tabulate sales discounts taken by customers for a year in total, we get a single figure, perhaps 0.5 percent of sales billed. But if we break the year into four quarters, we may get four different figures. This may be the result of seasonal or cyclical factors actually operating to produce different results in the different quarters, but it is entirely possible for a variation in the rate to arise from purely random factors in the general business system. The apparent variation does not always indicate that something is seriously amiss; every process or situation has some aspects of natural variation within it that should be no reason for concern. The really important fluctuations are those that arise from assignable causes, especially if they are subject to some control.

As we relate sales revenue to shorter periods, we would find greater variation, because daily sales may be affected by many and varied factors over the months of the year. However, different months will have varying numbers of weekends and different numbers of working days; the days of the week are not precisely comparable in sales potential, and days before or after holidays may be quite different from other ones. Shortening the estimating period may bring to the fore certain influences that are of little consequence in a longer period.

Thus, the issue of how long a period should be used for budgeting is one that can be answered only by compromise. The fact that data are noticeably affected by individual factors in the short period is reason to lengthen the horizon; but the unforecastable changes that may occur in a longer period make shorter forecasts more desirable. The problem is really one of what kinds of issues are important for the purpose at hand. Some forecasts cover long periods to raise issues that cannot be dealt with in short views; other forecasts require the kind of detail and recognition of specific factors that can be seen clearly only in short periods. One aspect of the time-period problem, however, ought to be considered here in some detail; this is the impact of the calendar on work schedules.

Work Schedules and the Calendar

For a company that operates on a five-day work week, a month may include from 20 to 23 working days; a six-day work week entails a 24-day to 27-day month, depending on the length of the month and on the day of the week on which it begins. In addition, there are various holidays during the year; these are not spaced uniformly, and there is a tendency to add one or more "days off" when holidays like Christmas or Independence Day fall on Friday or Tuesday. The existing calendar does not offer much chance of uniform short accounting periods. Perhaps the best that can be done is to use 13 four-week periods per year (a total of 364 days), adding a week to some reporting period every five or six years to catch up with the calendar. The four-week periods would each start on the same day of the week, and they would synchronize with weekly or biweekly reports and payrolls.

Typical Budget Periods

The operating budgets, or that summary of the operating budgets which is called the income budget (the profit plan, or the "view"), is typically established in general terms to cover a year, with more detailed estimates for departmental or divisional operations set up for the forthcoming quarter or semiannum. A year is short enough to permit fairly dependable projections of future events, yet it is long enough so that problems may be viewed in a reasonably broad context. Seasonal variations level out for the year as a whole, and other minor distortions are swamped out of the picture, so that the year forecast may be a good way to get a general idea of the program on which the company has embarked.

On the other hand, if the purpose is really to gain close control over specific operations, the budget period must be quite short. The variations that would level out over the longer period may need to be observed, and to the extent that they do not represent purely random and uncontrollable factors, they must be watched and dealt with. Fluctuations in the efficiency of worker activities or variations in the use of materials—which may appear unrecognized and uncontrollable in an annual forecast—are important factors to be recognized in the short period used for feedback and control purposes. Here, using a short period promotes close observation and careful analysis of all nonrandom deviations, and it may reveal places where methods may be improved or waste reduced.

For these reasons it is not uncommon to find both an annual projection and a shorter budget control period used in the business enterprise. Even weekly or daily comparisons of actual results against budget plans are not uncommon where a close watch on efficiency is important.

TRANSLATING SALES FORECASTS INTO PRODUCTION PLANS

We have seen that in order to use the sales projection to forecast production, we need a breakdown by products. The mix of styles, colors, or sizes is important if those variations of products will require different operations, different combinations in assembly, diverse materials, or other costs. Therefore, if the sales budget has not been prepared to show the required product details, there is good reason to try somehow to provide such data, even if it must be done by guesswork. This is especially relevant to inventory problems and strategies.

Decisions about Inventory

Inventories are important for management. They represent investment that has to be financed some way, and they represent risks of various kinds, yet they are useful in many ways. Still, management must be careful to use them efficiently. Planning the level of production ought to be done with a full recognition of inventory effects.

NEED FOR INVENTORIES—TIME AND SPACE PROBLEMS. Conceivably, a company might produce its products on a hand-to-mouth basis, turning out exactly what was needed to meet promised delivery dates. This would minimize the time between the start of production and the delivery of the product and thus reduce the investment over time in the costs of production. If this were possible, there would be no need for inventories of finished product, except for samples. Even materials and supplies could, in theory, be ordered for delivery at the precise time and place where they were needed. The only inventory would be the work in process, and that would be limited to the number of units actually to be delivered on a specified future date. The amount of work in process would be largely determined by the length of the production process.

However, in the real world the pipeline does not run so smoothly. Customer demand has a way of bunching up at uncertain times, and competition often forces promises of delivery to be made that can be fulfilled only if we have a backlog of goods on hand. Within the production process itself are other distortions and discontinuities. When the operating speeds of processing equipment are not uniform, the need to minimize idle facilities entails the maintenance of inventories between stages. This is even more apparent when we admit the possibility of unforeseen shutdowns or variations in flow rates. With respect to materials, there are other uncontrollable factors that require inventories to be carried. Outside suppliers are not always completely dependable in carrying out *their* operations; further, transportation delays, mistakes, or variations in quality may upset the smooth flow of materials into the production process.

Factors that fall within the firm and are subject to management control may be kept within desired limits; but forces and factors that operate outside the area of managerial control can only be hedged against by carrying "cushion" stocks of materials, supplies, or purchased parts to prevent tie-ups and confusion in our own operations. This raises a nice question of cost, however, for these cushions are not acquired and maintained without extra outlay. Hence, management must adopt some kind of a plan to maintain inventories to ensure the availability of materials, supplies, and products at some reasonable cost.

REGULARIZATION AND EFFICIENCY OF PRODUCTION. But there is another reason for carrying inventories—the desire to regularize or stabilize the rate of production. This is desirable not only to keep operating facilities in use for as long periods as possible, but also to maintain reasonably steady employment for the factory workers. This is especially true when there are weekly and monthly fluctuations in the rate of sales. To have workers engaged in overtime work every once in a while, only to be entirely or partly idle when demand is less, does not help to promote morale or to maintain a working staff. People who prefer steady employment (and most of them do) will move to other firms to achieve this; even though there is only limited mobility in the labor market, companies are obliged to provide at least a fair amount of stability in work and income. So even without any unusual or unforeseen changes, it may be desirable to build inventories in periods of slack demand to avoid overtime work and rush deliveries in busy periods. If the sales are expected to be steady (and normal) for the first two-thirds of a quarter but 30 percent higher in the last third, a production level of 110 percent of normal will supply the needed output at a constant rate of activity. But this assumes other factors to be irrelevant, which they seldom are.

It is possible that production at the rate of 110 percent is not so efficient as either 100 or 120 percent would be. Thus, there is an extra cost in operating at 110 percent, and it might be better to run at 120 percent for part of the time and then drop back to the normal 100 percent level, to average out to the required amount for the quarter. But this ignores the fact that it costs money to carry inventories; they require capital, space, and extra work. Further, there are risks in carrying inventories. Not only is there a chance of casualty loss (fire, wind, flood, and so on), but there are chances that goods may deteriorate, become less valuable or salable because of obsolescence, or merely because prices fall.

Of course, there is also a chance that prices may rise, and the firm may benefit from a speculative position; this might either intensify or offset the effect of other risks. In addition, there is the bad effect of delayed deliveries when inventories are too small. This may cause dissatisfied customers, lost sales, erratic production schedules (in the case of materials or supplies for the factory), or even idle plant and workers. All these costs, savings, and risks must be considered carefully when inventories are planned.

APPROACHES TO THE INVENTORY PROBLEM. Since there are so many possible combinations of these factors, different companies may take quite different approaches to inventory planning. Even within one company some stock items may be handled differently. For example, nuts and bolts or other small fastenings have low unit value, and there is not much risk of deterioration or price change. Such items are obtainable in regular channels without delay or difficulty, they are useful for a number of purposes, and they take little space. Under these conditions, the size of the inventory is not really important so long as there is space enough to store sufficient quantities to keep from running out of stock. But high space costs, perishability, or inconvenience may limit the amount of inventory to be carried, even to the extent of risking some loss of sales. In every case there is likely to be some compromise involved, and the decision involves marshalling resources in relation to expected events. Thus, a budgetary approach is part of the approach to inventory policy. Further, whatever policy may be adopted on inventory levels, it is essential to check actual results against the plan to establish whether or not the plan is being carried out and why.

THE CLASSIC INVENTORY MODEL. Perhaps the most scientific way to deal with the inventory problem is to establish standards for minimum stocks, reorder levels, and optimum purchase or production order quantities. The minimum level may be established by considering the risks of fluctuation in the rate of sale or usage; the reorder level may be set by adding to the minimum quantity the normal usage needs during the period of time probably required to place an order and get delivery of a replenishment lot. The purchasing or production ordering quantity would be determined by minimizing the average unit cost of carrying the resultant inventories.

The effects of establishing these standards for the management of inventory would be a pattern of inventory fluctuation as exhibited in Figure 3–1. Orders are placed when the quantity falls to the reorder level; since usage continues while the order is being filled, the stock is reduced to the minimum level before the replenishment arrives. The maximum level is reached when the order quantity is added to the

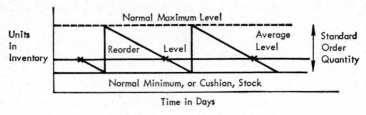

Figure 3–1. *Inventory fluctuation*

minimum, and the average inventory level is halfway between the minimum and maximum levels. In this simple case, the pattern is perfectly regular, because it has been assumed that the usage rate is constant, the order filling period does not vary, and the fluctuations guarded against by carrying the minimum stock do not occur. But the model does show the basic elements in the pattern.

THE SIZE OF REPLENISHMENT ORDERS.   The standard order quantity is established by noting the effect of different size orders on the unit cost of carrying inventory. Other things being equal, a larger order size will entail larger inventories, with concomitant cost effects. These effects are generally of three kinds, as shown in Figure 3–2.

Costs such as the purchase price or the standard cost of production will be the same per unit over a wide range of order sizes and inventory levels. These are represented by the horizontal line in Figure 3–2. Other costs, such as the paperwork required to place a purchase order, initiate a production order, or set up machines for a

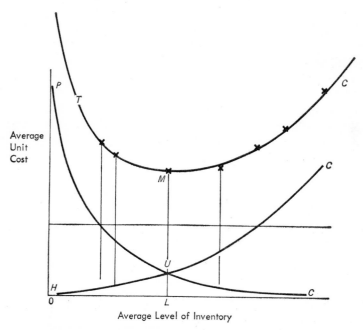

Figure 3–2. *The costs of carrying inventory at various levels*

given lot of product will be larger in total as volume increases, but they will actually decline per unit as more units are purchased or processed. These are represented in Figure 3–2 by the downward sloping curve, *PUC*. But there are still other costs that not only are larger with greater quantities, but actually grow at an increasing rate. Obvious items of this nature are risk factors such as spoilage, pilferage, and price losses. But storage space and interest on investment may be of this nature; added space is often available only at higher rentals, and additional funds are available only at higher rates. Costs of this kind produce a graph like *HUC* in the figure, curving upward to the right.

The combined effect of these patterns is the *TMC* curve, which is the sum of the various costs at each given inventory level. The minimum of the total unit cost curve (*M*) indicates the optimum level of inventory, the quantity *OL*. Generally, this optimum level is measured only in crude terms, because some of the costs are difficult to project (especially the risk factors); for practical purposes, this may be viewed as a guide rather than a precise answer.

RELATION BETWEEN INVENTORY POLICY AND BUDGETS. The decisions that are made about inventory policy depend upon factors that arise in the carrying on of production or purchase operations, and the operations of the purchasing or production department must be planned in terms of their effect upon inventories. The physical quantities to be produced in a given period depend upon not only demand, but also the way in which inventories are expected to meet the problems of fluctuating demands, risk factors, and cost control that lie between acquisition and ultimate use of the goods and services by the firm. The inventory problem must be faced in one form or another before the production budget can be firmly established. Both of these depend upon a clear perception of costs and methods to be employed which of necessity arises out of experience.

PROJECTING NEEDS FOR PARTS AND SUBASSEMBLIES. When the production estimate has been established in terms of units of finished product, it may be sent to those department heads who will direct the making of those products. Often, however, the production estimate must be expanded into estimates of assemblies, subassemblies, and parts required. A complex product like an automobile will often be turned out in different forms by combining various components—engines, transmissions, axles, and body parts. Production takes place largely in terms of these components; only the final assembly line deals with a complete product in final form. Even when there is only one way to put the final product together—for instance, in the case of small hand tools like hammers and screwdrivers—the parts may have to be made of different materials in separate places and by different processes. Production estimates are not useful unless they are broken down into specific operations and processes.

RELATING PRODUCTION FORECASTS TO OPERATION CENTERS. The details of production schedules are worked out for all the different operating centers. A program calling for the production of 10,000 electric washing machines, for example, will require a number of specific sheet metal parts, mechanical gear assemblies, agitators, timers, wire harnesses, electric motors, switches, lamps, and other items. Perhaps some of these things will be purchased from other companies (lamps, motors, timers). Those parts that have to be made in the sheet metal or gear-case sections of the company plant, however, may have to be specified in even more detail. The indicated parts requirements may be reviewed against existing inventories to arrive at schedules for producing different parts in economical quantities. In some situations this kind of detailed specification may have to be limited to a very short period of forecasting. The requirements may be hard to estimate (automatic options on autos like power window lifts, power steering, and so on), or it may be impractical to run out many parts in advance if they are bulky, heavy, costly, or fragile. Still other items (such as small screw-machine parts) may be purchased on a contract basis; needs may have to be worked out in very large lot sizes (an order for several million special screws is not unusual).

In any event, after considering inventory conditions, the supervisors in the various production centers can be told what kind of work load they may expect. These work loads may be stated in terms of parts or subassemblies. Bills of material and engineering specifications may accompany programs which specify general production levels in terms of man or machine hours of operation or in terms of the amount of materials to be processed. These projections will be used by the department heads to forecast operations, manpower, and costs.

THE JOB SHOP APPROACH TO PRODUCTION SCHEDULES

It is seldom possible to cover all the various situations in which different firms will find themselves by a single approach. Something specific about a single company often makes necessary some variation in method. A case in point is the production "job shop," such as a merchant foundry or similar special-order forging, heat treating, or machining processes. This kind of a firm has no "standard" product; its output is a collection of services defined only in very general terms. Those services are used to produce highly specialized products to the customer's specification. Production thus cannot be scheduled unless these contracts have been obtained. Such companies are often quite aggressive in seeking enough business to keep up some reasonable level of plant utilization. They therefore budget the plant activity and then sell the services thus made available—budgeting from inside-out, so to speak. In such cases, the sales personnel are engineering or production oriented, so as to be able to sense and translate the customers' needs into some use of their own company's production facilities. These sales people sell the production time of the plant, and their activities must follow from and fit into the otherwise scheduled production. This brings in some angles of cost estimating and projection of delivery times different from the approach used by "standard product" firms.

In a job shop situation, prices may have to be negotiated rather than set by market forces operating upon a standardized product. The accounting department is likely to be asked for special-purpose cost tabulations. For instance, it may be necessary for a sales representative to have some idea of the "average variable cost per machine hour" or to have a fairly clear idea of the "break-even cost." Although we are not quite ready to discuss these notions in detail, we may indicate their importance by observing that it may be desirable to accept orders even though the price per unit does not cover the total average unit cost. The firm may be better off to accept an order at a "shaded" price rather than to let facilities stand idle for part of the time.

Price Negotiation in Job Shop Sales

To illustrate this, suppose a sales engineer is considering a contract for the manufacture of 300,000 small bronze bushings. These could be turned out on semiautomatic screw machines that are presently scheduled at only half capacity to fill other orders. Fifteen of these machines are therefore available for a total of 300 machine hours per week. Past experience has indicated that the following schedule of costs (in current prices) is related to the processes involved:

Running costs per machine hour (power, coolant, recurring maintenance)		$1.75	
Standing cost per machine hour (depreciation, insurance, property tax, etc.)		1.69	
Machine cost per machine hour total			$3.44
Labor cost (attendant runs three machines)			
Labor rate $2.88 per hour	$2.88		
Fringe benefits 25%	.72	3.60	
Per machine hour			1.20
Supplies, small tools, miscellaneous			.60
Supervision, administration, building maintenance			.66
Total unit cost per machine hour of operation			$5.90

Cutting tools vary with the specifications and must be figured separately for each lot of product.

The nature of the material and the dimensions of this bushing indicate that they could be turned out at a rate of 135 per machine hour. This means that the total time required would be 2,222 hours for the lot (300,000 ÷ 135 = 2,222). Deliveries at the rate of 4,000 per week over a period of eight weeks could thus be expected. Of course, the sales engineer might negotiate for a little more flexibility in delivery, so as not to freeze up his whole schedule by using all available facilities on one contract.

As to the cost side of this deal, it might at first sight appear that since 2,222 machine hours will be required, the total cost of processing would be 2,222 times $5.90, or $13,100. Adding to this the cost of material (estimated at $9,000), the special tool cost (say, $350) gives a total of $22,450. This figures out to $7.48 per thousand pieces, and hoping for a profit, the engineer might quote $8.00 per thousand.

Even on a special order like this, however, competition does have some effect. Some other machine tool operator may have already offered a price of $7.00, and the purchasing agent may be entirely justified in refusing to order at more than $6.95 per thousand. Should the order be accepted at what appears to be a certain loss?

DECISION MAKING ON ADDITIONAL BUSINESS.   This situation throws into direct view just what must be considered in many management decisions. No one deliberately loses money if it can be avoided. But what are the alternatives available to the manager? If the order is not accepted, the presently unscheduled time of the machines will not be used. It costs money for machines to stand idle, and the question is really one of comparing two alternatives: (1) turning down the order and letting the machines (and the workers) remain idle for part of the time or (2) use the machines and the workers by accepting the order. The question is, which way is the firm better off? Taking a sharper pencil from his pocket, the engineer might consider by how much costs would actually increase if the order is taken. This would give him a chance to see whether a $6.95 price would leave anything to "cover overhead." The following calculation would ensue:

Cost of running time for the machines	$1.75 per machine hour
Labor cost per machine hour	1.20 per machine hour
Supplies, small tools, miscellaneous	.60 per machine hour
Total unit cost increase per added machine hour	$3.55

Multiplying by 2,222 machine hours, total operating cost	$ 7,889
Materials cost	9,000
Tools cost	350
Increase in costs if order is taken	$17,239

The available price of $6.95 per thousand will yield $20,850 of additional revenue that would not be had if the order were refused. The act of accepting the order puts the firm in a position to receive $20,850 more revenue by incurring $17,239 added cost. Thus, the company would be $3,611 better off to take the order than to reject it. Whether or not the order is accepted is then a question of whether this is the only chance the engineer has to sell the facilities of the plant.

RELEVANT COSTS. The foregoing illustration makes it clear that in making any managerial choice between alternatives, some costs change if a given course of action is chosen. These are relevant costs, because they depend upon and therefore have something to do with the decision. Costs that will be the same in total, regardless of the choice between alternatives, are irrelevant and should be ignored. The costs of having machines stand in the plant, supervision, administration, and building maintenance are irrelevant, because they would be exactly the same in total whether the order is accepted or not.

Of course, the engineer might bargain further, or he could ask concessions such as a guarantee against loss from materials price changes or assurance of future business. However, the cost data that apply to this decision are limited to the relevant costs—those that change in total amount with the choice that is made. This is in line with what has been said earlier, that plans are made by forecasting the results from various alternative courses of action and selecting the most advantageous one.

In this case, it might be said that production conditions serve to budget sales, because of the nature of the market and the generalized service that is being sold. Even so, the overall balancing of costs, capacities, and time factors is the same process as when production costs are forecasted from sales estimates. Budgeting is a way of thinking about problems, not a ritual of procedure.

BEHAVIOR PATTERNS ASSOCIATED WITH OPERATING COSTS

When a production supervisor is told what his department is expected to do in furtherance of the company operations, he will work out plans for the costs to be incurred in operating his own department. Before we get involved with the details of this, however, it may be well to follow up on the idea just set up: costs do not all respond in the same way to projections of operations. The idea that some costs change and some do not as we consider different alternatives may be expressed in somewhat more concrete terms; specifically, we want to consider how costs respond to changes in the rate of activity. There are variable, semifixed, and fixed costs; there are seasonal as well as erratic patterns in cost variation. Before we go very far into the forecasting of production programs, we need to study some of these cost behavior patterns.

Variable Costs

Costs that vary with (in proportion to) changes in the rate of activity are called variable costs. One example is the cost of materials directly traceable to the product—for instance, sheet metal used to make washing machine cabinets. Obviously, the more cabinets we make, the more material will be required; if price of the metal does not change and the efficiency in using the material remains constant, the sheet metal cost would be expected to vary with the number of cabinets made. This kind of relationship between cost and the rate of operations is exhibited in Figure 3–3. But the amount of a variable cost is not exactly proportional to volume in every case. Some sheets of metal may have imperfections or the efficiency of workers in using the material may vary. The points near the line in Figure 3–3 show

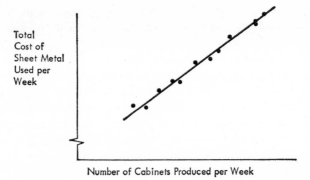

Total
Cost of
Sheet Metal
Used per
Week

Number of Cabinets Produced per Week

Figure 3–3

the costs for different weeks in which different volumes of production occurred. The points do not fall precisely on the line for the reasons noted. But the fact that they do fall so close to the line suggests that the deviation arises from random factors rather than from causes that can be identified and controlled. If the deviations had been large, there would have been reason to suspect that something was not as it should be. In such a case, one would seek the causes and try to correct the abnormal conditions.

UNIT VARIABLE COSTS.   Another way to look at the cost relationship presented in Figure 3–3 is to express it in terms of unit cost. In the present case, the addition of one unit to the production increases the total cost by a constant amount, as evidenced by the slope of the line of relationship. Since each added cabinet requires the same amount of

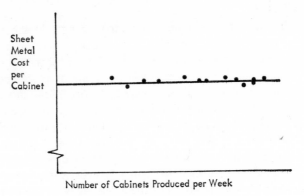

Sheet
Metal
Cost
per
Cabinet

Number of Cabinets Produced per Week

Figure 3–4. *Variable cost per unit*

added material, the unit cost of material is constant over the entire range. This is portrayed in Figure 3–4, which shows the same data (with the same random deviations) that appears in Figure 3–3. The fact that the unit cost is constant makes variable cost relatively easy to forecast; we need only multiply the expected production by the unit variable cost to establish the total costs to be incurred. Actual costs subsequently incurred should agree with this forecast. Deviations would be interpreted in a manner similar to that suggested earlier—small deviations may be dismissed as random, but large deviations suggest the need for explanation and correction of distorting factors.

Fixed Costs

In direct contrast to the kind of relationship just described, there are some costs that do not respond to changes in activity. Examples would be supervisory salaries, rent charges, or property tax costs. Although these items may change for other reasons (salary raises, changes in rates or valuations), there is little or no tendency for such costs to change when the volume of operations shifts up or down. Plotting the cost of the fire insurance, rent of buildings, or equipment (other typical fixed costs) would give a result something like that shown in Figure 3–5.

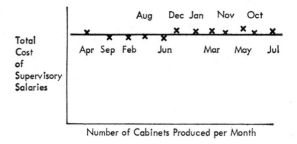

Figure 3–5. *A fixed cost as recorded for various months with different activity rates*

THE PLANNING HORIZON AND FIXED COSTS. One characteristic of fixed costs is that they tend to be related to the passage of time rather than to volume levels. Salaries, rents, insurance, and taxes are typically accrued for accounting purposes at a rate per period of time, because these costs are typically assessed in this way. This means that they may be viewed as being "time costs" rather than "activity costs," the latter group including not only variable costs but also those which respond only imperfectly to changes in activity rates or volume. The longer the period of time we are considering, the greater will be the total amount of fixed costs recorded for that period.

But time enters into the pattern of cost incurrence for fixed costs in another way. Some decisions encompass a long-range time horizon rather than the short periods of weeks, months, or a year related to operating budgets. In making long-range forecasts, the costs that appear to be fixed for short periods may actually be variable over the extended period. Since the scale of plant may be viewed as a completely open choice when one is thinking about the plants that might be built in the future, the rental, investment, or depreciation of those plants may vary in the same way as direct materials costs vary in the short operating period. This is the reason for the statement that "all costs are variable in the long run." But as used in this statement, the long run is a kind of "timeless time" unit used in forecasting for long periods, in which many alternatives are (and should be) considered. Typically, the firm faced with day-to-day operating problems must deal with an existing plant, an actual staff of supervisors, contractual agreements for rents, insurance, and so on. Thus, for day-to-day planning and operations, there is no point in the "long-run" notion. Useful as such an idea may be for longer range planning, it is irrelevant in a situation where certain costs are frozen at given levels or "sunk" in the sense that the decision to incur those costs was made in the past and cannot be changed within the horizon of daily operations.

FIXED COSTS PER UNIT.   Cost items that do not respond to changes in volume show a special pattern when considered on a per-unit-of-activity basis. Since the total fixed cost is the same at any activity level, dividing by an increasing activity rate produces a characteristic curve called a rectangular hyperbola, as shown in Figure 3–6. This kind of a cost pattern is the reason why people expect larger volumes of output to cost less per unit—the fixed costs are "spread" over more and more units, and the unit cost becomes less and less. Even with a large proportion of variable cost in the total cost, the unit cost would still fall as activity increased, because unit fixed costs decline, even though unit variable cost is constant over the entire relevant range. However, the fact that fixed costs per unit have a constantly declining pattern is really of small consequence in managerial planning, for we typically do not concern ourselves with unit fixed costs. The concept

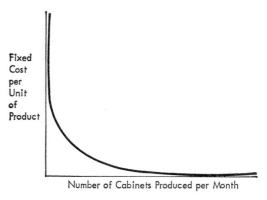

Figure 3–6. *Hyperbolic pattern of unit fixed cost*

of unit fixed cost is mathematically abstruse for most people, and we cannot plan fixed costs on a product unit basis. The costs that are fixed in total usually refer to services or assets that are acquired in large and indivisible quantities—buildings, leaseholds, even supervisors' salaries cannot be acquired in small quantities as needed for day-to-day operations. From a decision viewpoint, there is no such thing as a fixed cost per unit, because we cannot plan fixed cost incurrence on a unit of product basis.

Semifixed Costs

There are other, "intermediate" kinds of cost relationships met in practice. One of these is a hybrid: a pattern that is fixed over small ranges but variable in the broader sense in that the fixed "steps" in the pattern slope upward. This pattern of cost variation is sometimes referred to as a "step-cost" pattern. In terms of total costs incurred, this pattern looks like the chart in Figure 3–7. Examples of this kind of relation are facilities costs, like elevator operation in a building, or the semiclerical tasks like those of a receptionist or timekeeper. As the volume of traffic on the elevators increases, small changes can be absorbed by increases in number of passengers per trip or the buildup of a short waiting line. Let the traffic increase further, however, and a second elevator will be put in service, adding a block of relatively fixed cost to the total. Similarly, receptionists, timekeepers, and maintenance and other service personnel typically represent step additions to the payroll. One person does the work that needs to be done up to a point—beyond this, another person is added to the staff. The complications in this step pattern may be avoided by transferring the

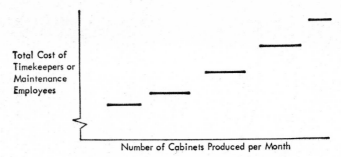

Figure 3–7. *Semifixed pattern, total cost*

worker to other tasks when the requirements are slack—as in the case of clerks at check-out stands in supermarkets. But it is not uncommon to leave a person assigned to a task even though he is not used with full efficiency. Then the step-cost pattern will appear.

The trouble with the step-cost phenomenon is that the work or service is not subject to close control. We may be unable to obtain a strictly efficient use of these facilities or services. There is no way to determine, for instance, just when the work load gets heavy enough to justify the addition of another worker or when it is possible to reduce the staff because of lessened activity. These decisions rest on probability judgments (which may reflect considered evaluation or mere guesses), and they are clouded by the fact that it is hard to see how changes affect results. How long can a waiting line behind a cash register get before the last customer or one of the others gets impatient and leaves without completing his purchases? The cost pattern referred to is illustrated in Figure 3–7 as if the steps were precisely determined, but this is often difficult to do.

If the step-cost pattern is reduced to unit cost form, it appears as in Figure 3–8. Each curve is a "unit fixed cost" for the corresponding step, and there are gaps between them. Such patterns of cost behavior make forecasting difficult.

Other Behavior Patterns

There are still other patterns of relationship between costs and the rate of activity of an operation. Sometimes there are combinations, such as might be exhibited in the charges for electricity consumption. Typically, there is some amount designated as a minimum charge; this may be a flat sum per meter per month, or it may be established by a count of rooms or electric outlets served by a given meter. This is the

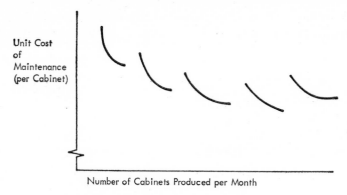

Figure 3–8. *Semifixed costs on a per unit basis*

same amount each billing period, once it has been set. However, the actual consumption of electricity may be billed at 9¢ per kwh for the first 100 kwh, 6¢ for the next 200, and 5¢ for the next 500; the excess over 800 kwh per month might be charged at only 3¢ per kwh. In such a case, the cost variability pattern for the electric power consumption related to the rate of activity might look like Figure 3–9.

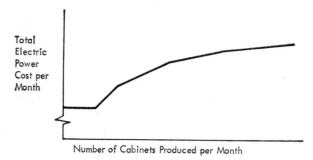

Figure 3–9. *Behavior of electric power cost*

Seasonal Variations

Up to this point we have been discussing costs as if the only factor that affects them were the volume of activity. This, of course, is not so. Some costs tend to follow the seasons of the year rather than the rate of activity. For a plant located where there are wide fluctuations in temperature, the cost of heating and air-conditioning might appear quite erratic when plotted against activity rates, but they could be quite systematic when viewed in a strict calendar year pattern. Figure 3–10 shows these relationships.

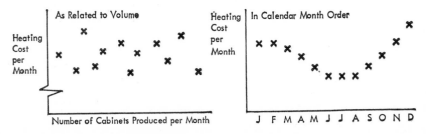

Figure 3–10. *Seasonality of costs*

Input Variables in Cost Behavior Patterns

Just as seasonal variations suggest that factors other than volume of activity will affect the costs incurred, it may well be that input factors may be much more important than the rate of activity measured in units of output. Certainly it is true that costs are determined by decisions which are more nearly tied to input than to output levels. But here again we see that purpose and circumstances are important.

The reasons for making forecasts may vary considerably. If the purpose of forecasting costs is to anticipate the need for additional financing or to see whether the desired output can be produced within some general limits of time or cost, a simple average relation between costs and output may be quite adequate. However, the purpose of budget forecasts is to specify management's expectations in such detail that feedback control can be effective. This makes mere aggregates of cost as related to output quite unsatisfactory. For control purposes, the cost behavior patterns must be closely defined in terms of factors that will anticipate the cost effects, rather than output that must *absorb* them. For this reason, many managements strive to relate costs to input factors; if conditions are not as was expected, the input factors may serve as "handles" with which to adjust the cost flows. These input factors are expressed in the quantities and prices related to cost incurrence; more specifically, they are weights, pieces, or other quantities of material, man hours of specified skills, or hours of machine operation, which are the things about which decisions are made and whose effects will ultimately be seen in costs.

With the emphasis upon input rather than output, a variable cost would be defined as one that varied with man hours or with pounds of material put into process. There would be an attempt to separate these input measurements from the effects of price changes. Changes in prices are not usually large enough to precipitate such questions in periods of short duration.

Mixed Costs

Recognizing the effect of different input variables on the incurrence of costs puts a challenging idea before us. Cost behavior is no longer to be viewed as a "natural" phenomenon, but as a resultant of factors and forces which ought to be isolated and studied if optimum decisions are to be made. Sometimes this is brought to management's attention by those cost behavior patterns best described as "mixed" costs, because they are the results of a mix of factors rather than a single one. One of these patterns appears in Figure 3–11. This

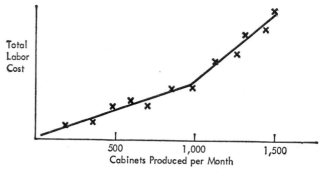

Figure 3–11. *Labor cost as related to activity*

relation might appear (as plotted) over a time period; the individual observations (one for each week or month of the period) indicate a relationship between labor costs and output. At the very least, this cost pattern will include the effects of regular-time earnings rates, overtime premiums, and shift premiums. It might also result from using less well-trained workers on certain jobs, differences in the quality of materials used, or changes in wage rates; anything that might affect the efficiency of labor or the cost of acquiring it could have an effect on the pattern. Only by allowing for distorting variables can some degree of control be achieved. In the present case, the kink in the cost pattern might be the result of overtime or shift premiums, and the separation of these from the rest of the labor cost

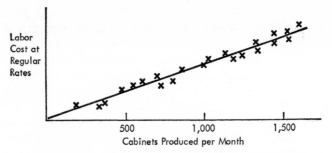

Figure 3–12. *Labor cost, excluding overtime premiums, as related to activity*

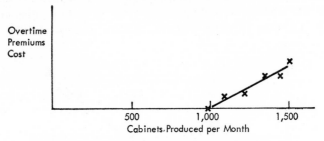

Figure 3–13. *Overtime premiums as related to activity*

might give two simpler patterns, each more clearly related to the control of work schedules (Figures 3–12 and 3–13).

Another and even more common mixed cost pattern is the one shown in Figure 3–14. This is sometimes called a "semivariable" cost pattern, but we will try to avoid this name—first because it is easily confused with the "semifixed" term we have already set up to describe step costs; second, because it is quite clearly a mixture of two elements in the cost pattern. One could observe such a pattern if a fixed cost element and a variable cost item were combined in a single account or classification, especially if the observed data were as shown in the chart. The cost appears to be variable, but an extension of the line of relationship cuts the ordinate at a positive level, suggesting that part of this cost is fixed. But one cannot be sure of this. What we need to do is to separate the two (or more) cost elements so that they can be handled with more understanding and by typical control procedures. Such analysis can often be done by fairly

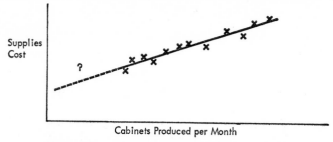

Supplies
Cost

?

Cabinets Produced per Month

Figure 3–14. *Supplies cost as related to activity*

simple methods, but partial regression analysis (of the kind used to isolate sales-affecting variables) can help to isolate such factors.

WAYS OF STUDYING COST BEHAVIOR

We have implied that one might conceivably expect certain kinds of response in costs as management changes the input factors. Without anything more than mere "common sense" to establish the judgment, it seems quite reasonable to say that the materials required for 20 product units should be twice the amount needed for ten. In many cases, we can rely on expectations of this kind. *A priori* judgments like this are quite common; they are things that people say they "know" from observation. One "knows" that a supervisor's salary will not shift upward from increases in the rate of activity over short periods of time, just as well as we may "know" that materials, power, and supplies will generally respond quite quickly and proportionally to changes in the rate of activity. However, when we seek evidence to verify such judgments, we may find things not expected in typical *a priori* conclusions.

An Example of Cost Behavior Analysis

The costs of operating a process may appear to have only a random relation to the activity rate, because of the presence of some variables overlooked in the first approach to the analysis. Consider Figure 3–15, a scatter diagram prepared for the management of a meat packing plant in an effort to get ideas about cost behavior patterns. The total costs of operating one section of the plant appeared to have no visible pattern of the sort we have been dealing with here.

In an attempt to make whatever progress that could be made, the

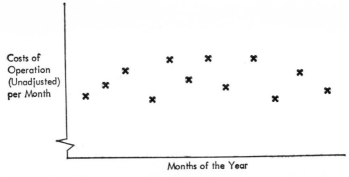

Costs of
Operation
(Unadjusted)
per Month

Months of the Year

Figure 3–15

management realigned the data so as to separate out the costs that were "obviously" (*a priori*) fixed and some others that were "seasonal" (related to notions about the weather). The remainder of the cost observations were plotted again as related to volume, the latter being expressed as the number of meat animals processed. The result appeared as in Figure 3–16. The reader can readily imagine that this

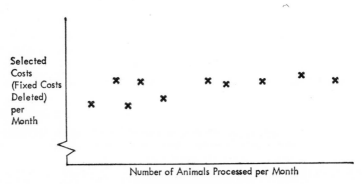

Selected
Costs
(Fixed Costs
Deleted)
per
Month

Number of Animals Processed per Month

Figure 3–16

result was rather disconcerting. Certainly some of the costs ought to have at least a minor relation to changes in volume.

Then a clarification was sought by using an input factor (man hours per month) to measure volume instead of mere output results. Plotting costs against man hours of operation (Figure 3–17) gave a pattern somewhat nearer to what was being sought—but it was still unsatisfactory. Then the costs were plotted against the total weight of

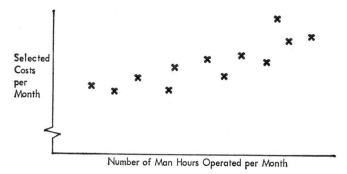

Figure 3–17

animals processed, to obtain the result shown in Figure 3–18. It was clear that a number of variables were operating in the cost pattern. However, the relationship between costs and the weight of the animals processed was closer than that for either number of animals or man hours operated. This suggested some peculiarity in the relation between man hours operated and the weight of animals processed. Tak-

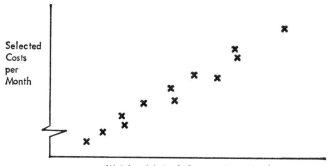

Figure 3–18

ing weekly data (in order to increase the number of observations over a short period of time) and comparing man hours operated with the weight of animals, the pattern shown in Figure 3–19 appeared. The obvious inefficiency in processing small weights suggested that numbers of animals and total weights of animals processed were not as closely associated as one might have expected. Comparing the weekly man hours and the weekly *range* of weights (heaviest minus lightest animal processed) exhibited a relationship which made it clear that a

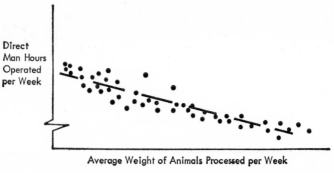

Direct
Man Hours
Operated
per Week

Average Weight of Animals Processed per Week

Figure 3–19

wide variation in the mix of individual animal sizes was responsible for the cost results.

Buyers had been shopping the market for bargains in the way of unclassified lots of animals of odd sizes and weights. The peculiar cost pattern was caused by this variation in the sizes and weights of animals. To reduce this effect (and to avoid the inefficiencies it caused), management decided not to change buying practices but to group the animals by size and weight before processing them.

Perhaps this same result could have come from careful observation of the operation in the plant. However, this did not occur, even though real effort was directed toward reducing costs and improving efficiency. Whether the result could have been obtained by one means or another is not really important. We may arrive at the understanding of cost controlling factors via *a priori* judgments, by casual or intensive observation, or by the analysis of reported data. But the *control* of costs can be achieved only after we are able to identify those factors which determine the cost.

Other Bases of Cost Behavior

The notion that input variables are the important ones to consider when forecasting costs is made even more clear when dealing with distribution or marketing costs. In the marketing area (selling, warehousing, shipping, and so on), many cost input decisions precede volume changes by a considerable margin. Salesmen are hired in anticipation of sales, not as a result of them. Planning the itinerary of a sales trip must be viewed not in terms of sales that will result from such travel, but in terms of mileage, number of days away from home,

13. The Chase Company produces and sells six models of radio and radio phonograph sets. The chassis, speakers, and cabinets are manufactured by the Chase Company in separate departments; record changers assembled into some of the sets, however, are purchased from other firms. Three chassis designs (x, y, and z), two kinds of speakers (I and II), and three makes of record changers (G, M, and R) are assembled into six styles of cabinets in various ways to produce the six models, as indicated in the following list of specifications:

Model No.	Cabinet	Chassis	Speaker	Changer
10	a	x	I	none
20	b	x	I	G
30	c	y	II	none
40	d	y	I	M
50	e	z	II	M
60	f	z	II	R

On September 30 the following inventories were on hand:

Finished Sets			
Model No.		Subassemblies	
10 460	x chassis,	310	record changers
20 730	y chassis,	170	G 170
30 640	z chassis,	270	M 340
40 690	I speakers, 470		R 190
50 520	II speakers, 180		
60 210	No cabinets are on hand except in finished sets.		

Expected sales of finished sets for October, November, and December are 2,000 model 10; 7,000 model 20; 3,000 model 30; 8,000 model 40; 4,000 model 50; and 1,500 model 60. The company wishes to maintain minimum inventory quantities as follows: 150 finished sets of each model; 200 of each style of chassis; 400 type I and 100 type II speakers; and 250 of each style of record changer.

Prepare a production schedule for the last three months, including purchases needed to complete that schedule.

14. A new item of stock was to be added to the Farwell Company's line of parts and accessories for its product. This item would be purchased, as made up to standard specifications, from outside suppliers. There was some question about how the items should be purchased, in view of the considerable spread in prices for various quantities, the limitations of inventory storage space, and the other factors involved. The firm operated on a six-day-week basis, and the requirements for this item would never be more than 100 per working day or less than 50 per working day; on the average, for 300 working days per year, the requirements would be 80 per working day. Regardless of the source

of supply to be used, it would take two weeks to place an order and get delivery, no matter what the size of the order was. To guard against errors and unusual conditions, the Farwell Company planned to carry a stock which would not, under ordinary circumstances, fall below 500 units.

Prices quoted on this item in terms of orders of varying quantity were as follows:

Size of Order (in Units)	Total Price
500	$ 1,000
1,000	1,990
1,500	2,955
3,000	5,880
8,000	15,520
12,000	22,800

The purchasing agent was eager to take advantage of the low prices for large quantities. In addition, he pointed out that there were certain savings in transport costs on the larger size orders. These costs were tabulated as follows:

Size of Order (in Units)	Transport Charge Per Order	Unit Cost
500	$ 36.00	$.72
1,000	48.00	.48
1,500	60.00	.40
3,000	96.00	.32
8,000	252.00	.315
12,000	375.00	.3125

The plant superintendent, however, argued that large ordering quantities inevitably meant larger inventories; these entailed greater provisions for storeroom space and more money tied up in stock, plus additional risk and handling cost. But the purchasing agent insisted that the cost of space and the investment were more than offset by the savings in purchase cost and that also to be considered was the cost of placing numerous orders over the year, each of which had to be received and put into stock separately—besides the fact that each invoice had to be approved and paid separately.

To solve the problem, the manager called on the cost department for certain estimates of cost to be used in making the decision. The cost of placing and clearing a purchase order in the purchasing department was found to be constant per order, regardless of its content. The figure was $4 per order. The cost of invoice approval and payment was $6 per invoice. Receiving and handling costs for this item were found to be $4 per shipment, plus 8¢ per unit placed in stock, plus 13¢ per unit withdrawn from stores. Storage costs were made up of insurance and taxes, estimated at 20¢ per unit stored per year; interest on the cost of inventory investment, 6 percent per year; plus a space charge that would depend upon the maximum size of the inventory. There had already been set aside an area of 4,000 square feet, the cost of maintaining which was estimated at 20¢ per square foot per year. Additional space could, however, be had at a higher cost. Six thousand square feet could be added in whole or in part at a cost of 21¢ per square foot per year; an additional area of 10,000 square feet was available in whole or in part at 22¢ per square foot per year; any additional space would cost 26¢ per square foot per year. The item in question required an average storage space of two square feet each, allowing for aisles and obstructions. The goods could not be stacked because of their height and their rather fragile construction.

What size of order should the Farwell Company adopt as the standard ordering quantity for this item?

15. The Sossmeyer Machine Company operates a machine shop in which various kinds of work are done on special order for various customers. The costs of operating the plant during the first six months of this year are summarized in the top half of the table on the facing page.

Miscellaneous statistical data collected for this period are shown in the bottom half of the table.

During July there were 20 working days and eleven holidays; 6,000 direct man hours and 5,000 machine hours were operated; materials cost $11,000, and the rest of the costs of operation were $41,540. Was this satisfactory? Show all calculations used to arrive at cost behavior patterns and relationships used to establish expected July costs.

Cost Items	Jan	Feb	Mar	Apr	May	Jun	Total
Direct materials	$14,000	$19,000	$21,000	$23,000	$16,000	$ 9,000	$102,000
Direct labor	23,970	30,140	33,020	40,680	30,510	16,950	175,270
Fringe labor costs	7,200	9,040	9,900	12,300	9,150	5,070	52,660
Power, machine supplies	1,800	2,700	3,000	3,300	2,100	1,200	14,100
Building occupancy	8,200	7,600	7,250	8,000	8,200	8,100	48,350
Depreciation, machinery	2,000	1,000	3,000	3,000	3,000	3,000	15,000
Repairs and maintenance	100	3,800	200	300	100	200	4,700
Totals	$57,270	$73,280	$78,370	$90,580	$69,060	$43,520	$412,080
Direct man hours	8,000	10,000	11,000	12,000	9,000	5,000	55,000
Machine hours	6,000	9,000	10,000	11,000	7,000	4,000	47,000
Working days in month	22	16 *	23	20	22	22	125
Holidays in month †	9	12	8	10	9	8	56

* The plant was shut down for three days in February to overhaul machines. The cost of making the overhaul was $3,400.
† Holidays include Saturdays and Sundays and shutdown time.
  There was a 10 percent wage increase for all direct laborers, effective April 1. An old machine, fully depreciated at January 31, was replaced with a new machine on March 1. No depreciation was charged during February, although the old machine was still in operation until March 1.

16. The present owner of The College Eatery acquired this business from a predecessor on January 1 of this year for $15,000, of which $10,000 was the agreed value of the furniture and fixtures, which had a then remaining life of 50 months. Of the purchase price, $8,000 was paid in cash, and $7,000 was financed through a chattel mortgage with interest at 6 percent.

The owner presents the monthly results tabulated from cash register information as shown on the facing page and the following additional information. He serves as manager, drawing $300 per month as salary. He employs a full-time cook, a full-time counterman, and a number of students who work part-time as cashier, busboys, counter help, and kitchen assistants. The lease on the building occupied by the firm runs for three years from the first of the current year. Much of the business is obtained from the use of meal tickets redeemable for $11 in meals but sold for $10 cash each. Meal tickets redeemed have been tabulated by months as follows:

Jan	$4,906	Apr	$4,664	Jul	$3,102	Oct	$4,796
Feb	4,422	May	4,840	Aug	2,992	Nov	4,620
Mar	4,092	Jun	2,684	Sep	1,056	Dec	4,356

Prices, wage rates, and inventories have all remained practically constant over the entire year. All bills have been paid when rendered, except that the rent for September was held over until October because of the small cash balance. The owner is pleased that he was able to retire $1,000 of his debt during the year, but he thinks that the results during the summer months (July, August, and September) are too poor to warrant keeping the place open.

(a) Draw up an appropriate statement of earnings by months (use totals to simplify the presentation of expense items).

(b) Using operating revenue as the measure of activity, identify the various patterns of cost behavior that can be established from the data given (rearrange expense data by months in ascending order of activity).

(c) Analyze (make a cost and revenue forecast) whether this business should be shut down in the summer months.

(d) Make any other comments you may think pertinent.

THE COLLEGE EATERY

Monthly Cash Operating Statement
Current year, ended December 31

	J	F	M	A	M	J	J	A	S	O	N	D	T
Cash sales of meals	$1,740	$1,700	$1,680	$1,760	$1,720	$1,760	$1,780	$1,680	$1,440	$1,560	$1,840	$1,240	$19,900
Meal tickets sold	4,360	3,720	3,840	4,920	4,300	3,440	2,740	1,640	160	4,640	4,460	4,140	42,360
Gross receipts	$6,100	$5,420	$5,520	$6,680	$6,020	$5,200	$4,520	$3,320	$1,600	$6,200	$6,300	$5,380	$62,260
Disbursements													
Food purchases	$2,480	$2,288	$2,160	$2,400	$2,448	$1,680	$1,840	$1,760	$ 960	$2,368	$2,416	$2,080	$24,880
Cashier	160	160	160	160	160	160	160	160	160	160	160	160	1,920
Gas and electricity	82	68	54	28	40	56	64	54	72	42	56	89	725
Cooks and countermen	760	720	720	760	760	640	640	640	560	760	760	720	8,440
Busboys, dishwashers	620	572	540	600	612	420	460	440	240	592	604	520	6,220
Kitchen help	930	858	810	900	918	630	690	660	360	888	906	780	9,330
Manager's salary	300	300	300	300	300	300	300	300	300	300	300	300	3,600
Heating	180	184	168	102	8	–	–	–	20	86	162	172	1,062
Rent	240	240	240	240	240	240	240	240	–	480	240	240	2,880
"Expense payments"	$5,752	$5,390	$5,152	$5,490	$5,486	$4,126	$4,394	$4,254	$2,672	$5,676	$5,604	$5,061	$59,057
Gross receipts tax *	122	108	110	134	120	104	90	66	32	124	126	107	1,243
Interest on loan				140							195		335
Principal of loan				500							500		1,000
Total payments	$5,874	$5,498	$5,262	$6,264	$5,606	$4,230	$4,484	$4,320	$2,704	$5,800	$6,425	$5,168	$61,635
Change in cash balance	$ 226	$ 78 †	$ 258	$ 416	$ 414	$ 970	$ 36	$1,000 †	$1,104 †	$ 400	$ 125 †	$ 212	$ 625

* Gross Receipts Tax is 2 percent of Cash Receipts.
† Decrease.

4

DEPARTMENTAL
BUDGET
SCHEDULES

We have seen how the basic estimating processes yield forecasts of sales and production volume and how operating charges may be related through various patterns to the rate of activity. Now we shall put these ideas to work. Sales and production forecasts will have set the work loads for various departments. By applying standard data about operating costs to those work loads, using various cost relationships that have been described, department managers will make up departmental budget schedules to show the accounting effects of these operations. In a production department, this will take the form of the number of parts, subassemblies, or units of product that are to be turned out. Even in a research department, the physical forecast of activity will list the projects and the kinds of work that will be carried for each. The operations of every department, section, or unit will be specified in some physical terms, and from this, each supervisor will be expected to indicate his needs in the way of man power, materials and supplies, services and facilities. Once these have been specified, it is easy to state them in money terms as expected operating charges for each department.

BUDGETS FOR LABOR COST

Analysis of Basic Requirements

Most producing departments of a manufacturing division of a firm will have to analyze the work load in some detail. Even very simple products require a number of operations. Typically, these are standardized to make use of specialization. Workers are trained to carry out these operations in stereotyped ways, using specified (and even specially designed) tools and facilities. Materials are purchased according to specifications that fit the processes to be carried on most effectively, and the whole process is systematized to achieve clear understanding and uniformity in the ways of doing things. This is a phase of managerial planning that we shall take for granted here; no matter what the operation, there ought to be some established way to do it. Otherwise, it would be difficult to achieve any well-defined uniformity in the parts that are to be assembled or any dependable level of quality in the product.

Sometimes these methods and procedures are mere products of experience, but more often they result from careful study and consideration of alternatives by people trained in the technical fields of engineering. This kind of planning—process analysis, work and methods study, and the setting of production standards—is a part of the technical field of production management. Such planning results in a set of standards which covers the ways in which operations are to be performed, the machines, tools, and materials that should be used, and the time that should be required to complete each productive operation as specified. These production standards are the building blocks from which the manager will build his operating charge and procurement budgets.

Direct versus Indirect Labor

In most manufacturing departments, a distinction is maintained between two classes of worker activity: direct and indirect labor. Direct labor is that kind of work which is easily and obviously associated with a given part, subassembly, or product. It is distinguished from work on general tasks that is not easily traced to or identified with parts or products. Such work is called "indirect" labor; it includes housekeeping or such facilitating activities as clerical work, general maintenance, and the like. To be able to identify direct labor work elements in planning, they are assigned operation numbers that mark them as different from other activities.

When we know the number of parts to be made, the direct labor costs and time can be calculated directly from the number of pieces or items. Listing the required operations and applying the proper standard rates will give direct labor time and cost for each part or item to be produced. Calculations like these are conveniently made by the use of a form such as is shown in Figure 4–1.

In addition to the direct producing operations, there will be other activities such as supervision, machine setup or maintenance, and moving of parts and supplies. Estimates for some of this work can also be made by use of standard times and procedures, as for example, setting up a machine so that it may be used to perform a specified operation on a given run of parts. Some other kinds of work may

Figure 4–1

CONVENTIONAL MANUFACTURING COMPANY
Direct Labor Budget
Department 8, month of April 19—

Part No.	Opera- tion Number	Produc- tion Re- quired	Standard Hours per Piece	Total Hours	Rate	Total Cost
D-3714	9031	1,500	.100	150	$1.60	$ 390
	9033		.320	480	2.80	1,344
	9034		.144	216	2.80	605
	9012		1.48	222	3.10	688
R-3812	9003	1,800	.067	120	2.00	240
	9033		.320	576	2.40	1,382
	...					
Total direct labor				4,578		$12,018

require less systematic approaches; maintenance work may be estimated on merely a time basis, hours per day or per week. Sometimes various functions are combined for convenience or simplicity, as for instance when a single person does both setup and machinery maintenance. In any event, the indirect labor costs are projected separately to make the forecasts more meaningful; they are typically collected in a form such as that shown in Figure 4–2.

Figure 4–2

CONVENTIONAL MANUFACTURING COMPANY
Indirect Labor Budget
Department 8, month of April 19—

F.T.E. *	Task or Operation	Hours Required	Rate	Total Cost
1	Machine setup	172	$2.40	$ 413
.5	Maintenance	86	1.75	151
1	General helper	172	1.60	275
1	Foreman	172	3.20	550
				$1,389

* F.T.E. means "full-time equivalent"—work load for one person.

A nonmanufacturing department would probably set up its labor estimates largely in the form of an unclassified work-force budget. Certain departments that operate to provide services for other operating units may be of this kind; for example, the boiler room, power plant, and storeroom do not have "direct" labor costs because they do not perform actual operations on product parts or assemblies. Their personnel needs would be summarized in schedules like Figure 4–2, perhaps labeled "personnel requirements" or "planned staff needs."

Personnel Budgets

Combining all the data shown in the direct labor and indirect labor budgets gives an index of work force required for the firm as a whole during the forthcoming period. It would be possible, for example, to tabulate all the working time required for given operations, and from these set up estimates of how many full-time worker equivalents would be needed to meet these needs. This may be done in such a way as to see how the available work force could be best used by effecting transfers or combining certain separate tasks into full-time operations. But it may also be set up to compare the total needs in the way of manpower with the indicated available staff (those now on the payroll who are expected to remain). This would show how many additional workers of various kinds would have to be recruited from outside sources. Such data are very useful to personnel officers in planning promotions, training programs, transfers, or new hires for the forthcoming period. For this reason, the personnel department will want to see a tabulation of the departmental needs for manpower derived from the departmental labor budgets, direct and indirect. Perhaps the budget of the personnel department itself may depend to some extent upon these projections, especially when training or recruitment programs must be changed to meet additional needs. And in any event, it is of some importance to be able to see where opportunities are developing for transfer, promotion, or reclassification of workers. Information of this kind is valuable in making assignments of workers to tasks that fit their abilities and aptitudes, for the most efficient use of the personnel resources of the firm.

"Fringe" Labor Costs

The data shown in Figures 4–1 and 4–2 are, of course, not the total costs of employment. There are taxes, occupational hazards insurance, vacation and holiday pay, and other costs associated with employment. Typically, however, these are estimated along with the "other service and facilities costs," such as electric power, repairs, and depreciation of equipment. Often these items can be estimated as percentages of the basic payroll costs, but even then it is better not to get these "fringe" items mixed up with direct labor or other payroll estimates. The reason for this will be better seen when we discuss the issues that may be raised by departmental labor forecasts.

Issues Raised by Department Labor Budgets

When the initial tabulation of man hour requirements has been completed, it may be found that man hour requirements do not produce full-time assignments for the available employees. If, for instance, 1,431 man hours of a certain level of skill will be required for production and the work time scheduled for the month is 172 hours, this indicates that slightly more than eight full-time equivalents will be needed (1,431 ÷ 172). There may be no concern over the fractional result; if it can be taken care of by small amounts of overtime or by transfers to or from some other departments, the matter may be ignored. But there is always the possibility that such transfers may not be feasible. Then there is a question of whether some worker(s) may be left unemployed for part of the time or whether some should be asked to work overtime to fill in the production schedule.

TRANSFERS AND OVERTIME. In the interest of morale, the department manager may prefer not to have his staff transferred back and forth from other departments; but certainly it would hardly be fair to add a worker who would be only partly employed because of the mechanics of the schedule. Thus, it may be better to plan for overtime work to absorb the excess. In the case just cited, however, this does not necessarily solve the problem. Eight men working 172 hours each (the normal schedule) would provide 1,376 man hours, which would mean that there would be 55 man hours of overtime to spread over eight men. This would average to just under seven man hours of overtime work per man. However, that simple solution might break up the efficiency of operations; once a run of parts is set on a machine, it may not be wise to break it off just any place, for there is an "economic" length of run. The supervisor must judge how the odds and ends of jobs and time are assigned to the workers. He must avoid an uneconomic use of time and machines, but he must also avoid an excess of overtime work for any one man. Although overtime premiums are extra income for workers, nobody wants to work overtime beyond a certain level. It is up to the supervisor to work out such problems for the best results, all things considered. Often the answers are less than ideal, but they will at least be better than the confusion that would have resulted from letting things take their course.

OTHER WAYS OF ROUNDING OUT A SCHEDULE. There are other managerial questions that may arise from a consideration of labor requirements. Often there are alternative ways to perform certain kinds of work; it may be possible to use machines with similar but not identical characteristics on a given task. Of course, these different methods could involve different time allowances, yet it might be desirable to sacrifice a little labor efficiency to gain better utilization of equipment or to complete the assigned production within a given time period. Problems of this kind can be quite complex, and in some large plants it may be desirable to assign such planning and scheduling tasks to a specialist group or a production control office.[1] Frequently, however, the foreman or department supervisor is expected to work out problems of this kind for his own department without the help of staff people such as planning and control units. Obviously, the department foreman will then make his estimates in such a way as to avoid trouble of one kind or another, and he may depend on rough calculations, guesswork, or judgment when help is not available.

MATERIALS AND SUPPLIES BUDGETS

Sometimes the production process is so stereotyped that the department manager may have little or no choice as to the kinds of materials to be used or the way in which they are to be handled. Mass production frequently requires planning outside the actual producing departments. A foundry in which motor blocks are cast for automobile engines typically is not able to specify the materials it will use. If the metal is to be delivered in a molten state from another department, that other department or some planning agency will determine material specifications. Nevertheless, there may be some variation in the product which permits, or even requires, variation in the kinds of materials used. In such a case the department manager may be asked to specify the kinds and amounts of material required for production.

This is especially likely to be the case when there are options as to how materials are to be used. Sometimes what would otherwise be waste may be used for additional product; occasionally it is more economical to produce things in groups that permit advantageous combinations of materials usage. Or it may be that the work force can be more effectively handled if the foreman is allowed some discretion in the specification of materials or if he is allowed to schedule various sequences of product runs so as to make the best use of equipment. In such cases, the department foreman or supervisor may have to make

---

[1] Mathematical techniques such as linear programming can be useful in such situations.

decisions about materials. He will at least have to indicate the quantities of given materials required, but he may also need to specify the kinds of materials to be used or even to state when they will be needed.

Obviously, the nature of a departmental materials and supplies budget will depend upon the degree of autonomy given to the foreman or supervisor. Assuming that the department foreman is expected to make the whole decision about what kind of materials shall be used and the way in which it will be handled, the materials and supplies budget will be quite detailed and specific. Such an estimate sheet appears in Figure 4–3. Often the materials and supplies budget estimate is carried out at the department level only in physical units; price data are added by the purchasing office. This is especially likely to be the case with materials whose prices tend to fluctuate widely. It may even be necessary to have the "priced" list of material requirements returned to the department head for review, for changes in price or available substitutes may raise the question of whether changes are desirable.

Figure 4–3

CONVENTIONAL MANUFACTURING COMPANY
Materials and Supplies Estimate
Department 8, month of April 19—

Part or Assembly No.	Scheduled Output	Material Stock No.	Material per Unit Output	Materials Required (Units)	Price (Estimated)	Expected Cost
D 3714	1,500	XD 1406	12	18M	$100/M	$18,000
		RB 1842	3	4.5M	160/M	7,200
		XC 1908	10	15M	72¢ ea.	10,800
		RB 1844	6	9M	23¢ ea.	20,070
R 3812	1,800	XD 1406	12	21.6M	100/M	2,160
. . .						
Total direct materials						$49,320
Supplies: Lubricant		1b 3300		10 gal.	$ 2	20
Wire		76 2306		7 coils	30	210
. . .						
Total supplies						$ 540
Total materials and supplies						$49,860

PURCHASE BUDGETS

The purchasing department is the company's official connection with its supply market. The task of keeping up with the various conditions and developments in such a market is sufficiently complicated to warrant having a staff group perform the functions related to purchasing. When this is done, operating supervisors no longer have the responsibility to establish the details of purchase contracts. Rather, the supervisor indicates the quantities and sometimes the specifications of materials that will be required, and the purchasing department takes over the rest of the task of negotiating for the needed items. The materials and supplies budgets prepared by the different operating departments are, of course, an important source of information to the purchasing staff. But the issues to be met by the purchasing decisions may be quite different in different situations.

Various Approaches to Purchasing

If the purchasing staff is informed of the needs for given materials or supplies, they may place orders for these things whenever requests are made. The purchases budget may serve as an indication of these needs far enough in advance to permit extended negotiation and/or search for the required items. This might permit quantity purchases to cover an extended period, with deliveries scheduled to fit the production plan. This might reduce costs and avoid otherwise higher inventory levels.

SYSTEMATIC PURCHASING. But items for which there is more or less continuing or recurring need may be ordered "for stock." An inventory may be maintained at such a level as will meet ordinary requirements for 30 days or so to ensure the continuity of operations while an order is placed and delivery is obtained. The systematization of purchasing in this way avoids the direct dependence of the purchasing staff on the purchase budget for placing orders.

STANDARD ORDER QUANTITY. The quantity of the item to be purchased in a given lot is the standard order quantity. This is established so as to minimize the total average unit cost of the stock item in question. This minimum total average unit cost (like but not identified with the pattern shown in Figure 3–1) would be affected by several groups of factors. The first group, including price concessions on large quantity orders, savings in transportation and handling costs with larger orders, and the costs of negotiation and paper work for a purchase order would make the average unit cost lower as the size of the order increased. Another group of costs would tend to increase the average total unit cost as the size of order was expanded. These would operate largely through the higher average level of inventory and would include interest on investment, storage, insurance, and the risks of deterioration or price declines. Still a third group of costs might have little or no effect in raising or lowering the average total unit costs; these are costs that vary in direct proportion to the number of units purchased—like putting the items into stores or issuing them. The regular invoice price would fall in this category if there were no quantity price concessions. These variable in total, fixed per unit costs are really irrelevant, except as they may affect interest on investment or other cost measures.

REORDER LEVEL. The reorder level is the level of inventory at which an order ought to be placed to avoid running out of stock. This is often set by the total usage over the order filling period (estimated average daily usage multiplied by the number of days required to place and fill an order). If an order is placed when the stock falls to the reorder point and the average rate of usage and order filling time are correct, the inventory should fall to zero just before the replenishment order is delivered. To guard against errors in these estimates, however, companies may establish a minimum level, or cushion, so that the chance of being out of stock is reduced. Thus, the inventory level would fluctuate between the minimum level and a maximum— determined as the reorder quantity less usage over the order filling period plus the standard purchasing quantity. The average level of inventory in units would be halfway between the minimum and maximum levels.

This kind of system works very well if the minimum level, the reorder level, and the standard purchasing quantity are worked out carefully. But even if the purchasing process is thus systematized, it may still be worthwhile for the purchasing staff to know the projected needs for materials and supplies. If the usage rate suddenly increases, it may be necessary to increase the minimum and reorder levels of inventory; if the quantity of an item used in a month or a quarter becomes large enough, it may be worthwhile to study the advantages of purchasing on contract delivery or in larger quantities. Further, even if there are no questions raised with respect to inventory levels or purchasing quantities, it is advantageous to forecast the costs of materials and supplies to be purchased, if only to foresee the financial drains that these purchases will involve. Therefore, the materials and supplies budgets are transmitted to and are studied by the purchasing staff to insert prices and to forecast delivery dates and cash required to pay for the items that will be purchased.

SPECULATIVE PURCHASING.   Occasionally, purchasing is handled on a quite different basis. Things that represent a large portion of the product or operating cost, whose prices may fluctuate considerably over a period of time, may be purchased on a speculative basis. This means that the purchasing agent and his staff will attempt to reduce costs by contracting for such items over fairly long periods, sometimes months in advance of the actual need for them. There are various reasons for this kind of purchasing. It may be a matter of bargaining for a better price through contracting for a large quantity, even though delivery may have to be spread out over a period of time to avoid heavy storage and holding costs. If the price is low enough, it may be advantageous to carry the heavy inventory, even at some risk and extra cost. Timing purchases to take advantage of low prices may save the firm large amounts of money.

Speculative purchasing requires fairly precise estimates of needs. It is foolhardy to acquire large quantities of an item without knowing when and how much of it will be needed. Therefore, in such cases where this kind of buying is to be done, it is essential that the purchasing staff should be informed of the plans and needs of the operating departments in as much detail as possible. Even if advance buying is not specifically aimed at price savings (for example, where the contract for a year's supply is placed at the beginning of the year to ensure regular deliveries and dependable service from the supplier), it is still essential that the purchasing staff be well informed on the projected needs for the item. Hence, the purchasing department needs the information shown by the departmental materials and supplies budgets to be able to plan its activities and programs.

Combining Estimates

The purchasing staff will tabulate the requirements of various departments to find the total amount of a given item that will have to be purchased, because the same items may be used by a number of producing departments. The purchasing staff will also review the departmental plans to be able to make whatever comment or recommendation that might improve the quality, cost, or smoothness of operations. Should there be substitutes that ought to be considered, or if there are advantages to be had in changing sources of supply, the purchasing department will suggest changes that appear to be advantageous. In the last analysis, however, the operating manager should have the final say on specifications and quantities of an item to be used in his operations, for he is responsible for the product output in terms of quality, quantity, and overall cost.

The materials and supplies budget is thus seen to have a "side function" like that of the direct labor budget—to inform the procurement agency of the expected needs for carrying on operations. The specialized operations of personnel or purchasing departments themselves may be based upon and forecasted from the other operating budgets. The same is true of various other service or staff departments, such as tool design, inspection, or plant maintenance.

GENERAL SERVICE, OR "OVERHEAD," BUDGETS

Costs related to direct labor, materials, and supplies are only part of the total cost of carrying on operations in a department. True, they represent a considerable part of the total cost of operations; but there are other items, such as electric power and light and various other outside services or facilities costs that need to be considered. These "other" costs may be quite varied in nature; some may be variable, others fixed or mixed in behavior pattern, some related to personnel or labor costs, others related to materials and supplies; and some related to equipment. For this reason, it is useful to discuss them separately in these terms.

Labor Related Costs—Fringe Items

A number of overhead, or "indirect," costs are related to the cost of labor required to carry on production. The employer's share of payroll taxes imposed by state or federal governments and insurance premiums to provide against occupational diseases and accidents represent costs of this kind. They are often charged as direct percentages of payroll or some part thereof. Other fringe costs are associated with paid holidays, vacation, overtime, or other premiums paid for work done at unusual times, such as on Sunday or on a night shift. There are also bonuses paid for output or efficiency beyond a specified level. There may be health or life insurance programs or supplementary retirement or gain-sharing plans that represent partial or complete contributions by the employer. These various fringe labor costs may represent a sizable part of the labor cost of operations.

LABOR ASSISTANCE COSTS. In addition to the items already mentioned, there are costs associated with labor cost in a supervisory sense, such as the cost of work done by timekeepers, custodians, general maintenance people, helpers, or clerks. Labor assistance costs are incurred because of and largely for the benefit of direct workers;

the amount of labor assistance usually is closely associated with direct worker activities.

ESTIMATING LABOR RELATED COSTS.   Costs like those mentioned may be estimated individually, or they may be arrived at by averages or percentages. To make this more specific, consider a direct production worker who is entitled to be paid for six holidays in the year (New Year, Memorial Day, Independence Day, Labor Day, Thanksgiving, and Christmas) and also for two weeks' (ten working days) vacation with pay. This is a total of 16 days for which the worker will be paid when he is not working; these amounts are earned (and are really to be included as costs) for the days the man actually works. Allowing 104 days for Saturdays and Sundays and 16 paid holidays, a year contains 245 working days. The cost of the paid holidays and vacations is thus 16/245, 6.53 percent of the base earnings. Thus, when a man has worked 40 hours, he has earned 2.6 hours of paid holiday or vacation time; if his pay rate is $2 per hour, the amount of $5.20 should be accrued toward pay for holidays and vacation periods. Usually, overtime hours are ignored in figuring this accrual, for the vacation is related to the basic work week and will be paid in those terms. In preparing the budget, of course, it must be remembered that some people will be needed to continue the essential work while the regular personnel are on holiday. (This, too, may involve special premiums!) Of course, the employees' rates of pay may change, so that the vacations may be taken at higher rates of pay than that in force when the accrual was made. But this is usually ignored in budgeting paid holidays, and it is adjusted at the time of vacation or holiday, rather than trying to anticipate the possible changes in rates of pay.

SOCIAL SECURITY PAYROLL TAX COMPUTATIONS.   Social Security taxes do not lend themselves to simple forecasting techniques. The current (1969) Federal Insurance Contribution (employer *and* employee) is 4.8 percent on earnings up to $7,800 per year; the unemployment compensation tax may be 2.7 percent state and 0.4 percent federal, levied on the first $3,000 of earnings. Since a good many employees will earn more than $7,800 during the year, assessments in the earlier months cause the cost to be recorded in those months. Since payments are less (perhaps nil) in the final months when earnings accumulate to more than $7,800, it may appear that there is no tax on the latter part of the year's operations. Further, the state portion of the unemployment compensation tax is subject to experience rating, and the rate is not always 2.7 percent, even on the first $3,000. These conditions may cause some confusion, and an attempt to forecast them precisely may take more effort than the added information is worth; but they cannot be left out of the forecast unless we are willing to overlook an important part of cost.

It can be argued that these taxes are actually a general levy against payroll and that their amount could logically be accrued over the entire payroll cost for the year at a level average annual rate, set to recognize and spread the total tax costs over the dollars of payroll. This would serve to tie payroll taxes to the incurrence of labor cost and to fix responsibility for them on the aggregate use of labor rather than to the question of whether the legally set accrual has or has not been accomplished. An illustration may be useful.

Suppose that a company has 70 employees, who are expected to earn a total of $580,000 in the forthcoming year. Of this, $550,000 may be judged to be subject to employers' F.I.C.A. tax. This estimate is higher than might be expected, since the taxable wages are only $7,800 per employee, indicating a total tax base of $546,000. But some people may leave the firm's payroll after they have earned $7,800, and those hired to succeed them will also be included in the tax base. Similarly, the amount subject to state and federal unemployment compensation taxes may be judged to be $230,000, which again is (for similar reasons) more than the specified $3,000 earnings per employee times 70 workers. On the basis of these estimates, the employer's F.I.C.A. tax will be 4.8 percent of $550,000, or $26,400. The state unemployment compensation tax rate may be 1.8 percent; this, plus the federal rate of 0.42 percent makes the total unemployment compensation taxes 2.2 percent of $230,000, or $5,060.

Matching the total estimated employer taxes against the expected total payroll ($31,460 ÷ $580,000) gives an expected average rate of 5.424 percent. This rate may be used to accrue payroll taxes for the shorter periods within the budget, so that a payroll of $40,000 budgeted for a month or a four-week period would be accompanied by a "payroll tax cost" of $2,170 in that budget. In the early months of the year, the charges for payroll taxes would be less than the disbursements; but this will be offset by accruals of taxes in the latter part of the year, when less or even no disbursements are made. The error over the year will be too small to affect financial data materially. For operating purposes—especially for budgetary control and internal reporting purposes—it is simpler to view social security taxes as if they were a flat percentage of payroll.

OTHER FRINGE COSTS ACCRUED ON THE BASIS OF PAYROLL. There are other costs more or less directly associated with payroll accruals, as for instance occupational disease and accident insurance. Premiums on such policies are typically billed by the insurance companies on the basis of a rate applied to estimated payroll. The premium paid is subject to adjustment when the actual payroll for the quarter or year is known. This establishes the correct charge, and the additional premium or refund is paid. A good way to account for such charges is to accumulate them by average rates, as was done with payroll taxes. Certainly they can be budgeted in no better way.

Materials Related Costs

Some operating charges are tied to the handling or processing of materials. The cost of supplies, certain kinds of transport, or handling labor may be closely allied to the weight, size, or number of units of materials used. Some of the costs incurred in receiving and store-rooms would be estimated in this way, but these would be budgeted by the stores department. They might be included in the materials costs as a storeroom service charge, based on volume or dollar amount of materials issued. Also, in an operating department, there may be costs related to materials usage, such as helper's time or devices used to handle or protect the materials being worked on. In a few cases, materials usage may actually be the best indication of department volume, and it may be preferred to man hours or other input measures.

Machine Operating Costs

There is no reason why there cannot be a separate tabulation of machine operating costs in preparing a departmental budget. Machine costs are likely to be more closely related to machine hours than to man hours, for it is possible for certain types of semiautomatic machines to operate without attention or with only occasional adjustment by operators. In such a case, man hours of operation may be an unsatisfactory way to project such machine costs as power, adjustments, repairs, and the like. In addition, machines may be idle part of the time while workers are busy with other tasks, and it may be essential to forecast machine hours of operation in order to estimate machine costs.

Fixed Costs Related to Machinery and Services

It should be noted that some of the costs related to machines are independent of usage. Such costs as property taxes or leasing rentals do not fluctuate with a machine's rate of use. Although it is possible to regard depreciation as a form of wear and tear, expected to be higher when equipment is used more intensively, the typical situation is more likely to be that depreciation is viewed as a time cost rather than an activity cost, based more on obsolescence than wear. Therefore, depreciation, like property taxes, rentals, and insurance against casualty damage, would tend to be regarded as part of the "standing" cost of equipment rather than part of the cost of operating it.

There are other fixed costs that ought to be budgeted within the department, such as the costs of certain kinds of facilities that may be rented or owned, such as office machines; there may be costs of service contracts associated with various equipment items. There are likely to be salaries of assistants or staff helpers—even the department manager's own salary. Such costs should be budgeted by the department in which such services are used. It may be argued that those items are to an extent uncontrollable; but there is something to be said for having a supervisor know what costs are, even if he is not held accountable for their incurrence. A typical form to summarize "indirect costs" (all operating charges except direct labor and direct materials costs) appears as Figure 4–4.

Fixed Costs Originating Outside the Department

It is not always clear just when and how one should depart from the strict text of controllability in budgeting. For example, it is common practice to treat the cost of space as a cost that should be allocated to each department. Certainly the supervisor ought not to think that space is a free good; he should recognize that heating, ventilating, and other building operation costs (elevators, drinking fountains, locker rooms, lunchrooms, and a wide variety of other facilities and services) are provided and used by operating personnel. These costs must be covered in the operations of the firm, and the behavior of many different people can influence the amounts of such costs. Yet it should also be recognized that the task of estimating and controlling building occupancy costs must be centered where decisions are made about those costs. Typically, this is the building maintenance manager, who should estimate, plan, and control this activity. Production department supervisors do not have this responsibility except through the indirect channels of "good citizenship." There is good reason to budget costs only in terms of their control, even to the extent of making internal charges at standard rates for services used, so as to carry the costs to the operating unit in

Figure 4–4

DEPARTMENTAL COST ESTIMATE FORM
INDIRECT COSTS BUDGET

DATE _____, DIVISION _____, DEPARTMENT _____

Item	Basis	Quan-tity	Rate	First Quar-ter	Second Quar-ter	Third Quar-ter	Fourth Quar-ter
Indirect labor	Schedule						
Fringe labor cost							
Overtime premiums							
Materials handling							
Supplies	Schedule						
Electricity							
Phone and travel							
Outside contracts							
Depreciation							
Amortization							
Supervisory salaries							
Office and clerical							
Wages, salaries							
Fringe costs							
Other, miscella-neous							
Cost transfers							
Space charges							
Repairs and main-tenance							
Other							
Miscellaneous							
Totals							

meaningful terms. Although such procedure would permit internal "gains and losses" (which would have to be handled properly for financial reporting), it might assign responsibility for producing the service separate from responsibility for use of it. In any event, a department manager cannot be expected to budget that which he cannot plan, and he cannot be held accountable for that which he cannot control.

BUDGETING VERSUS COST MEASUREMENT

To follow the line of thought just outlined would mean that some —perhaps a fair number and amount—of the costs traceable to given operations (from the viewpoint of accounting measurements of product cost) might be kept out of the operating budgets. Those costs which originate in some service center and are later prorated to the operating departments (personnel department, building maintenance, power production, and the like) would be budgeted separately, and the control of costs would be left to those managers who had initial responsibility for them. The operating departments which use those services would thus not consider them in the preparation of budgets, and those costs would not be included in the reports of the operating departments. There is merit in this point of view, but some companies prefer to set up standard charges for internal service transfers and to insist that each department or division "stand on its own feet" with respect to costs chargeable or traceable to it.

Imputed and Allocated Costs

Costs like depreciation or patent amortization, interdivisional but intracompany charges for interest on investment, may also be charged against operating departments. In some cases, the "costs" may be imputed or alternative costs rather than actual disbursements or expenditures; for instance, interest on investment may be based on current appraised values of facilities and the indicated overall cost of capital as judged from market conditions. The argument over whether each managerial unit should be set up to know and bear its own costs is not easily settled; there are reasons for maintaining a number of positions. The point is, however, that there should be at least some care to distinguish between those costs which originate in the decisions of a manager and those which are part of the environment in which he operates. So long as the distinction is maintained, the incidence of control will not be disturbed by whatever recording arrangement seems desirable to top management.

Dealing with cost prorations is not always free from serious error. Sometimes, perfectly rational intentions have misleading results. For example, the company that is concerned about payroll costs in its branch offices, or that feels that the central office "overhead" is really incurred for the benefit of employees, may choose to prorate general office overhead to its branches on the basis of dollar payrolls. This has the "obvious" advantage of stressing payroll costs heavily, and it may prove effective; but if some branch offices start off with more slack in their payroll situations than others, the relatively easy reduction of payrolls in some branches may result in an *increase* of overhead charges to branches in which the payroll was in tight control to begin with. Thus, inefficiency may be inadvertently subsidized by the results of a cost proration that may have seemed entirely reasonable when first set up. Unless management is willing to spend considerable time and money to make prorations of cost really sound and effective, it may be better to refrain from charging a department with any cost responsibility unless complete autonomy can be established.

CAPITAL EXPENDITURE REQUESTS

Outlays for major overhauls or for replacement of equipment constitute a special kind of budget problem. The area of capital budgeting is a complex one, and it cannot be covered adequately in a brief discussion of operating budgets. Yet this area is not easy to separate from day-to-day planning; it ought to be given some recognition at this point.

Budgeting the regular operations of any enterprise inevitably raises questions about methods: the possibility of using tools instead of bare hands; the addition of jigs and fixtures to make work more systematic and efficient; the use of different machines for doing some kinds of work; wasting a little material or a bit of machine time to save more in labor cost. All these alternatives and others will tend to be considered frequently. Such issues ought to be settled by careful study, but no one solution can be entirely right for all situations. A good "methods" or standards department will establish optimum ways of doing things. These results should be codified in procedures manuals. A foreman or supervisor ought not be allowed much latitude to depart from "standard" practices. Occasionally, however, a new piece of equipment becomes available or a new material appears on the scene, and the question of how the work ought to be done is reopened. When this happens, it is essential to get proper information about the proposal, so that it may be evaluated.

Tabulating Savings

If the change involves a capital outlay, the relevant data are tabulated in a special form, so that the kinds and amounts of savings may be specified along with other facts about the investment. This form, of which Figure 4–5 is an example, may be used for the kind of review that has been described above.

Figure 4–5

CAPITAL EXPENDITURE PROPOSAL

Item or Function_____

Date_____

Division and Department_____

Approved by_____

Recommended by_____

Prepared by_____

Existing equipment		Proposed equipment
_____	Description	_____
_____	Make or source	_____
_____	Installed cost	_____
	Revenue advantages	
$_____	Output	$_____
_____	Quality	_____
$_____	Totals	$_____
	Cost advantages	
$_____	Labor costs	$_____
_____	Fringe labor	_____
_____	Setup costs	_____
_____	Maintenance	_____
_____	Repairs	_____
_____	Tools	_____
_____	Supplies	_____
_____	Power	_____
_____	Spoilage	_____
_____	Property taxes	_____
_____	Insurance	_____
$_____	Totals	_____

Summary

Total cost or saving	$_____	Total cost or saving	$_____
Interest on investment	_____	Interest on investment	_____
Next year's salvage loss	_____	Next year's salvage loss	_____
Income tax effect	_____	Income tax effect	_____
Other	_____	Other	_____
Net, after taxes	$_____	Net, after taxes	$_____

Comments

Often the department manager will prepare the capital expenditure form, suggesting that the expenditure should be made. This would involve the collection of data concerning the operating costs, investment outlay, and other items concerning the proposal. Presumably, these figures would show some financial advantage for the proposal. There may be other advantages, such as better quality of product or improved worker morale; these would be reported in the comments on the form. All this information would be discussed by the foreman with his immediate superior, usually before the proposal is sent to the budget officer for review.

Proposals thus received by the budget officer will be classified as to the amount of investment required, the kinds of results expected, and the urgency of the proposal as indicated by the recommendations made. Some of the proposals may be approved without further ado, but others may require attention of other officers.

There is a close relation between capital expenditures and efficiency of operations. Often the kind of equipment available restricts what can be done about product quality, output, or cost. The problem is, of course, to decide when added capital investment should be made. This is ordinarily a matter of comparing savings in operating cost (or added value in quantity or quality of output) with the capital expenditure required to obtain those advantages.

Since the use-life of equipment covers a relatively long period of time, it is necessary to compare costs and advantages over the use-life rather than for only one year. In such long-term comparisons, the interest cost of capital must be considered; future revenues and costs are discounted to present worth by compound interest methods to recognize the effect of interest cost. Since the use-life interval replaces the single year as the planning horizon, calculations of annual depreciation are of no consequence, except for their effect upon income taxes. The present worth of the whole stream of after tax revenues and costs that is in excess of the current outlay for the proposed capital improvement (the net savings) indicates the desirability of the project. The procedures used—and the various shortcuts that are sometimes substituted for them—are somewhat complex and are left for more comprehensive works on capital budgeting.

Financial Review

Most companies implement the pattern of authority for expenditure by a system of approvals. For instance, a foreman or department supervisor may be empowered to make commitments for purchases up to $50. A section chief might have authority for expenditures of up to $500; a plant superintendent or district sales manager, up to $2,000; and a division chief, up to $5,000. The president's authority may actually be limited to $25,000, and only the board of directors could initiate larger outlays. This, of course, means only that the purchasing officer would be instructed to honor requests within these limits; actually, the right to contract for the corporation is usually very severely restricted in the interests of internal control.

But even then there may be requirements for certain kinds of review and approval. This is the case with capital expenditures. Usually, capital expenditure means an outlay of more than, say, $1,000 for equipment or facilities expected to remain in service for perhaps three years or more. The actual definition is set by each company for itself. But typically, every capital expenditure is reviewed by some representative of the finance division, so that some analysis is assured and modest safeguards are applied. Thus, the figures on the form will be checked for consistency and validity; they may be compared with past operating reports or engineer's figures. Some proposals may be sent to the company's engineering staff for review of technical features and reasonableness. But the finance department will apply some form of overall check in the fashion of computing the proposed return on investment, the payment period, or a present worth computation. This kind of calculation will make it a bit easier for the company finance committee or treasurer to decide which proposals should be approved. Some of the proposals may be referred to upper level management or the president; it is possible that large investments may require approval of the board of directors.

The importance of capital expenditures makes them worthy of more extended analysis than can be included here. The reason for bringing them into this discussion at all is to indicate their importance as elements in the planning process which may affect the operating cost estimates and to indicate the kind of financial planning that will have to be done in preparing the projected statement of position as one of the budget summaries.

SUMMARY

This chapter indicated how work loads derived from extensions of sales or production forecasts could be converted into financial terms. We applied different kinds of standard times and quantities related to various productive operations to the work loads and priced them to arrive at dollar amounts.

Various kinds of direct and indirect labor requirements can be forecasted from standard operating times to indicate the amounts and kinds of skills that will be needed. These amounts may be put into the form of manpower requirements or a personnel budget, used by the personnel department to do its planning of recruitments, promotions, transfers, or other staff adjustments. These would be worked out to achieve acceptable results in terms of overtime work or schedule changes to make optimum use of available workers. Transforming manpower needs into labor cost is accomplished by pricing at appropriate wage rates. The result is a labor cost budget showing the labor cost of all work that is to be done in each department over the budget period.

Materials and supplies budgets are set up in similar fashion to show kinds and amounts of items that will be required. These data are reported to the purchasing department to be used in planning procurement operations. Such plans necessarily involve attention to inventory position. There are various kinds of relations that are useful for decision making in this area; systematic procedures, contract purchasing, and speculative buying have effects upon the purchase budget. Stated in terms of expected prices, the departmental materials usage becomes a materials and supplies cost schedule, which, combined with the labor cost budget and the general service, or "overhead," budget, produces the total department cost budget.

The general service, or overhead, budget is a collection of a number of different cost items. There are labor related costs, which are typically forecasted as percentages of payroll cost; materials related costs that may follow materials usage rates; and other variable and fixed costs which originate in the department. The departmental budgets may also include allocated charges for building space, general management costs, or even imputed charges for interest on investment. Although a department manager cannot logically be held responsible for costs over which he has no control, it is often thought that he should at least be aware of the cost of services and facilities made available to him. But there is a real need to maintain careful distinctions between controllable and uncontrollable costs. The reader may find it of interest to look back at Figure 2–3 and compare the cost classifications in the departmental cost report with the budget procedures described here.

Capital expenditures are also a part of the budget program. Although such proposals may be initiated at various times, they should be considered in the preparation of operating budgets. Often the desirability of capital expenditures may be brought to light when the future pattern of operating costs is reviewed. In any event, capital expenditures are subject to specified review and control procedures, and they must be considered when budget summaries are made, especially in terms of their effect on cash flow and financial position.

QUESTIONS

1. Why are budgets prepared by managers and foremen at the departmental level rather than in the controller's office by qualified staff people?

2. What is included in a departmental labor budget? Is there a good reason for separating direct labor estimates from indirect labor projections?

3. What interest does a personnel officer have in departmental labor budgets? Would the labor budgets be useful in projecting personnel department activities?

4. What are fringe labor costs? Would these generally tend to vary with direct labor dollar costs or with man hour activity? Is this because they depend upon labor costs, are caused by direct labor costs, or are calculated that way? Indicate exceptions if any.

5. Why are overtime bonuses not an unalloyed blessing for the employee? What advantages does overtime have for the employer?

6. What responsibility does a department manager have with respect to materials and supplies acquisition? Does the separation of storekeeping functions and purchasing authority reduce this responsibility?

7. Distinguish between a departmental materials and supplies budget and a purchase budget. What relations are there between them?

8. What is speculative purchasing? When is it desirable? What kind of cooperation is required to make it effective?

9. What is meant by level rate Social Security accounting? What objections are there to this procedure? When might it produce less useful results than "actual cost" recording?

10. Give the arguments for and against having a department budget include the costs of all services made available to the department, regardless of their nature or source. What kinds of cost give trouble in this connection?

11. What is a capital expenditure request? What kinds of data are typically considered in such requests? Why is this kind of cost given special treatment in budget systems?

12. In one department of the Modern Package Company, the operations consist of making sacks for packing fruits and vegetables. The sacks are made by cutting the cloth into rectangles twice the size of the

sack, folding these rectangles once, and sewing one end and one side of the folded material.

Based upon orders actually on hand or contemplated for the months of April 19—, the company has scheduled production for that month (20 days, eight hours per day operating time) as follows:

	Type A	Type B	Type C
Finished size (inches)	11½ × 5½	23½ × 8½	33½ × 15½
Cut size (inches)	12 × 12	24 × 18	34 × 32
Number required	114,000	48,000	72,000

The italicized dimension is the length of the open end of the sack. Since the sacks will be sewed or tied after filling, the open end of the sack must be a selvage edge—the original woven edge of the material. The cut size makes allowance of ½″ for seams; hence, the cut size of the cloth is slightly greater than twice the finished size of the sacks.

Sacking material is purchased from outside supply firms in 100-yard bolts and comes in three widths: 24″, $9.60 per bolt; 36″, $13.80 per bolt; 48″, $18.00 per bolt.

The manufacturing operations in this department consist of three steps: cutting, sewing, and bundling. Details of these operations are given below.

Cutting is effected by handwork. The experience of the company indicates that the cost of cutting materials lengthwise of the bolt of cloth is 1.80 cents per running yard of cut. Transverse cutting, however, costs 2.70 cents per yard of cut.

Sewing is done by two types of machines. These have slightly different characteristics, as determined from past experience.

	Size of Sack					
	A		B		C	
Machine Type	99-a	101-b	99-a	101-b	99-a	101-b
Output, sacks per hour	100	105	75	80	50	60
Power cost per hour of operating time	51¢	69¢	54¢	72¢	72¢	90¢
Thread cost per 100 yards stitching	60¢	60¢	60¢	60¢	60¢	60¢

There are twelve 99-a machines and eight 101-b machines in this department. Each machine is operated by one person, who is paid on a piece rate basis as follows:

PIECE RATES PER 100 SACKS SEWED, BY MACHINE TYPE

Size	99-a	101-b
A	$1.80	$1.62
B	2.40	2.25
C	3.60	3.24

The third step in the operations of this department is bundling, which consists merely of tying the finished sacks in stacks of 100 sacks each. This work, the movement of goods within the department, cleaning and oiling of machinery, and other miscellaneous tasks are performed by two helpers who are paid a flat rate of $2.00 per hour. These men work eight hours every day that the department is in operation; if they work more than eight hours in any day, they are paid overtime premiums on a "time and a half" basis. The department foreman is paid a flat salary of $500 per month, regardless of the rate of activity in the department.

On April 1, the storeroom contained the following:

13 bolts 24″ cloth	$ 124.80
22 bolts 36″ cloth	303.60
17 bolts 48″ cloth	306.00
90 spools sewing thread (1,000 yds. each)	145.00
450 coils bundling twine	540.00
32 quarts lubricating oil	48.00
	$1,457.40

The inventory planned for the end of April is 21 bolts 24″ cloth; 35 bolts 36″ cloth; 15 bolts 48″ cloth; 100 spools of sewing thread; 100 coils bundling twine; and 28 quarts of lubricating oil. No bundling twine or lubricating oil will be purchased in April.

It has not been found economical to use scrap pieces of material to make sacks. Therefore, only one size of sack is cut from any given bolt of material.

Prepare:

(a) A schedule to be sent through the comptroller's office to the purchasing department showing the amounts and kinds of materials which should be acquired for this department during April. This schedule should be set up with respect to the most economical method of using the materials for the planned production.

(b) A statement of the costs to be incurred for the operation of this department for the month of April. This statement will, of course, be incomplete because data for depreciation, light and heat, repairs, and maintenance are not given.

5

BUDGET
SUMMARIES

The first tangible products of budget planning are the departmental schedules of planned costs and revenues and the procurement programs expressed in personnel, purchases, and capital expenditures budgets. These forecasts are formal tabulations of management decisions; in them, each department head has put together in concrete terms his considered judgments about what will be done in his area of jurisdiction. While considering these plans, managers will have conferred with their associates and superiors to fill in gaps in their information or experience and to check the desirability of proposed activities; there will be a certain amount of give and take in the working out of details.

We need something more than this, however. The knowledge and abilities of departmental managers are limited to a relatively narrow area of activity. The plans that they will set up will necessarily be based on their immediate problems and circumstances, and it is not likely that they will be very much concerned with the fortunes of the firm as a whole. We need some overall check on the combined programs to see whether they will in fact meet the needs and maintain the position of the enterprise. This check is provided in budget summaries: the profit plan, the financing budget, and the position budget. In this chapter we shall see how departmental data are summarized, reviewed, and finally approved by top management when they have met the tests of profitability, financial feasibility, and expected financial position.

THE CONTENT OF BUDGET SUMMARIES

Profit Plan

Budget summaries look very much like the typical financial reports of an enterprise. One of them—the projected income, or profit plan —looks very much like a statement of earnings, except that it presents the effect of proposed transactions, not actual ones. But it shows, as the difference between projected revenue and expense, the measure of expected earnings which represents the net economic accomplishment to be achieved. The amount of expected earnings that will be left after distributions of interest, income taxes, and dividends measures the net growth of the firm. The amount of earnings and the growth of the firm are two basic tests of business effectiveness.

Financing Budget

However, earnings and growth do not tell the whole story of business progress. There is a considerable area of decision making and planning with respect to acquiring and using funds. All the transactions of the firm involve some aspects of financing (past, present, or future), and a sizable amount of managerial planning has to do with raising funds and controlling their use to pay for goods and services acquired or to settle obligations for other things. Somebody in the management team must be concerned with the problems of cash flow and financial arrangements. Typically, this involves planning the finances as related to the revenue, operating costs, and the several procurement budgets; this is usually directed by the chief financial officer (who may have the title of treasurer, vice-president of finance, or controller). Also, this financial plan (the financing budget) must be reviewed by the top management group or the budget or finance committee, as may be indicated in the particular firm. This financing budget will look very much like a Funds Statement or a Statement of Receipts and Disbursements; of course, it refers to proposed activities instead of the actual transactions that would appear in conventional accounting reports.

Position Budget

Even when a company can raise all the cash needed to carry on its operations, it is possible to do this in ways that leave the firm in various states of financial strain or stability. For example, there could be overinvestment in receivables, inventory, or plant; there may be too high a level of debt as compared to shareholder equity or too much financing on short-term bases as compared to long-term arrangements. There may be failure to grasp opportunities for modernization, expansion, or diversification; or there may be idle funds not used effectively to produce income, because their presence was not anticipated. All these conditions emphasize the need to balance various aspects of asset management, capitalization, and the effective use of capital. They are usually portrayed in a conventional position statement, and they may be similarly projected in a "position budget," as this is expected to appear at the end of the budget period.

PREPARING THE PROFIT PLAN

The profit plan is prepared by putting together all the data in the sales budget, the departmental schedules, and the procurements budgets; but this has to be done in such a way as to pick out those data which will effect profits. The budget officer and the financial staff will have to make certain computations to transform the estimates made by the operating management (sales, production, and service departments) into revenue and expense figures. But before this is done, there should be some review of the plans prepared by departmental managers to make sure they are reasonably complete and consistent. Typically, departmental schedules are forwarded to the budget officer's staff as soon as they have been reviewed by immediate superiors.

Budget Officer Review

When budgets for the departments are received in the financial division, they are first reviewed to locate any obvious errors or omissions. Sometimes a comparison with the corresponding estimates of last quarter or last year may help to check for differences. Sometimes it will be useful to form some judgment of the reasonableness of the plans. We have already suggested that sales forecasts would be checked against outside or independent sources to see that no large unexplained differences exist. A sales estimate calling for a substantial increase in volume without any concurrent price changes would hardly be a reasonable expectation if general business conditions and the industry are declining. A plan for cost reductions would also be subjected to independent checks of acceptability. The budget officer may be of real help in raising questions of this nature, before the figures are put into the larger context of company-wide decisions.

Revenue Estimates

Often the sales budget is made up only in terms of orders expected from customers. In some situations this is the same thing as sales, because immediate delivery from stock is anticipated. But a sales budget may need to be translated from an "orders" basis to a "delivery" basis to provide a useful revenue estimate. This is especially to be considered if business is obtained on a contract basis, with deliveries staggered over some period of time. A sale is more than a mere contract to sell, and delivery is an important step in operations as well as for revenue determinations. Therefore, the budget officer or his staff may need to review "sales" forecasts to make sure that deliveries are likely to be made promptly and that "sales" are not mere additions to the backlog of unfilled orders. This will be even more important when we try to use sales data to forecast cash collections from customers.

Another factor to be considered in making revenue estimates from sales budget figures is that various revenue deductions need to be taken into account. If sales have been forecasted on the basis of nominal or typical prices, subject to trade discounts, losses on uncollectibles, freight or damage allowances, price concessions for special reasons (quantity or lost discounts, end-of-season price cuts, and the like), these factors must be allowed for in establishing figures for revenue. The patterns established and the basis for estimating revenue adjustments may be reviewed by credit, traffic, or other staff personnel in the sales division. These people can use various methods based on experience to estimate such items. But somebody must make sure that these adjustments are considered if they have a real effect on the amount of revenue.

Although it is possible to establish such revenue adjustments individually, it is not always easy or even essential to make separate calculations for each item in this group. Sometimes a flat percentage to cover the whole pattern of adjustments may be used, especially if the amounts are relatively small and fairly consistent in behavior. However, when there are individual fluctuations in behavior of different items as related to time of year, cyclical patterns, territorial divisions, or lines of product, it may be necessary to make allowance for the individual revenue adjustments so as to show their effects.

We should note here that revenue adjustments are not always viewed in the same way by managers. Sales discounts are treated even by some accountants as "financial expense"; we should not be too critical if managers consider them as alternatives to collection expense and hence "collection costs." Losses on uncollectible accounts are not really costs in any direct sense—the *costs* were charged as costs of goods sold when the "sales" (which turned out to be nonexistent) were booked. But alternatively, one may accept a certain amount of collection shrinkage or loss if it achieves a saving of collection cost or if we get more net revenue by accepting some uncollectible business. Hence, it may be quite correct to consider uncollectibles as alternative costs for management purposes; as such, they should be planned and controlled. Credit managers ought to budget discounts and uncollectibles as parts of the plan of credit management.

Divisions of the Revenue Budget

Revenue budgets are often more meaningful if they are set up to show revenues separately by products, territories, or classes of customers rather than as mere enterprise totals. This may be of even greater importance if there are choices to be made as to how much emphasis ought to be given to particular products, territories, or customers. They may be crucially important if they reflect differences in expected costs and profit margins. The revenue data must be arranged in whatever way will serve to raise pertinent and significant questions for management's attention. In making decisions about such classifications, the budget officer will often call attention to current trends or conditions that may suggest possible changes in established practices and procedures.

Thus, the profit plan will show revenue data that give effect to the sales department's expected operations in terms of the revenue expected to emerge from product or service deliveries, by four-week, monthly, or quarterly periods of time. These would be adjusted to reflect the force of discounts, uncollectibles, price concessions, and allowances. Further, there might be various subclassifications (to show separately the revenue from various product lines, territories, or customers carried into the summary profit plan) if there are conditions that require top management review of revenue determining decisions.

Expense Estimates

The starting point of all expense computations is the cost incurred when resources or services are acquired. These costs are traced to current period operations as the related services are made available to customers. As a matter of convention if not of actual fact, some costs are almost immediately transferable to expense. Payroll and current costs of transportation or communication incurred by selling and general administrative departments are usually so regarded. Some items that are recognized initially as assets (inventories, prepaid rentals, or equipment costs) may become expenses as soon as they become assignable as current period costs of carrying on selling or administrative activities.

Manufacturing costs, however, are not expense until the related units of product are released to customers via delivery against sales. Thus, there is a flow of manufacturing costs through the category of operating charges—costs of carrying on manufacturing operations— into inventories of work in process, parts or subassemblies, and finished stores. Only when the goods are sold is the cost associated with them recognized as expense—cost of goods sold. For reasons that will be presented shortly, it is common practice to use a standard cost of goods sold to complete the profit plan, even when manufacturing operations are budgeted in detail.

Standard Unit Costs in the Profit Plan

A standard unit cost is an expected cost—it is that unit cost that would result from performing given operations under specified conditions of prices, methods, and efficiency. Although standard costs are often established by the use of engineering or statistical techniques, they are no different as to logical content from the unit costs that were used to establish departmental cost estimates. With planned output at 100,000 units and an expectation of using three pounds of material for each product unit, we would certainly budget for 300,000 pounds of material. The only reason for a different forecast would be that we expected some change in the efficiency of using this material. Further, if we estimated the cost of this material to be 60¢ per pound, a total of $180,000, we would be assuming a certain market situation and purchasing arrangement that would yield such results. Every expected cost has within it an anticipation of surrounding conditions that may cause variances; every forecast reflects some anticipation of conditions and postulates some level of efficiency. Thus, every expected cost is a standard cost of a kind—it reflects the typical condition and is therefore a norm from which to measure. But the use of standards to establish product costs in the profit plan and the position budget has other advantages.

PRACTICAL ADVANTAGES IN STANDARD COST. In addition to the logical necessity for using standard unit costs to budget departmental costs, there are practical advantages in the use of aggregate standard costs in budgeting. To convert a manufacturing cost estimate into an expense figure, it is essential that those costs be expressed in product units; only in terms of finished products do the firm's manufacturing efforts reach the market. To make this conversion would require that the whole process of cost accounting be applied to the budget to provide a cost of goods sold figure; this, for obvious reasons, would be impracticable. Thus, the use of standard product costs to measure cost of goods sold and to state expected inventories is the only practical way to establish such figures.

MANAGERIAL ADVANTAGES. One important aspect of all business data is its relevance for decision making. Some things are very important and meaningful with regard to one level of decision but unimportant for other levels. The building maintenance manager must recognize seasonality in controlling the costs of heating and ventilating; he must recognize that certain kinds of repairs must be effected and certain inspections and adjustments made at specified intervals. Similarly, a manufacturing department foreman is concerned with the possible substitutions of materials for personnel effort or of manpower for machine time; he must schedule certain work in particular sequences to meet delivery dates or to allow time for preventive maintenance work to be done. Costs which result from such departmental decisions are important at that level. But at the level of strategy and policy— where the tests of budget summaries such as the profit plan are applied—these costs may be relevant only in the sense that they ought to be covered by revenues.

In order to focus attention on the proper issues, it is desirable to free the profit plan from as much internal and subordinate detail as possible. Thus, using standard unit costs to measure cost of goods sold for different product lines has advantages. But even more than this, the use of standard unit cost has the merit of stating expense in overall terms, without raising tedious questions of internal efficiency at lower organizational levels. That is, by assuming in the profit plan that expected performance will be attained in the subordinate levels, top management may concentrate its attention on the overall issues of enterprise policy that the profit plan should evoke.

At the same time, the use of standard costs makes it possible to make specific allowance for variances which arise from known sources of inefficiency, such as new and untrained workers or substandard materials. If those conditions are known or expected to exist, the budgeted variances can be used to recognize their presence. Thus, it is admitted that those factors make the standard cost unattainable and that operating management has accepted this situation. The allowed manufacturing variances (representing expected actual costs in excess of standard) will be accumulated and presented among the summary figures of the profit plan as a profit reducing element arising from inescapable inefficiency. For obvious reasons, the total amount of manufacturing variance should be relatively small.

Certain other kinds of cost may have to be dealt with in preparing expense figures for the profit plan. There may be research or development costs to be expensed (or deferred); whether or not these will appear as assets or expense items in the summary budget is decided on the same grounds as will be used in making up the actual income report at the end of the period. Similarly, there may be certain obligations to be incurred (pension contributions, liabilities for product warranties, or customer service, for example) which the budget officer may have to include if the departmental schedules do not already reflect them. Probably the most important task of the budget officer with respect to the profit plan is to be sure that all elements related to or likely to affect the operating net margin for the period are taken into account in forecasting revenue and expense for the budget period.

Income Projection

The profit plan tends to emphasize the operating net margin—the difference between revenue and total operating expense. Various types of ancillary income or expense (for example, investment income and unusual or nonrecurring costs) may be included in the profit plan, but these are addenda to the main pattern of recurring and regular operations. If such items are included in the profit plan, they ought to be clearly distinguished from operating items.

The amounts of income taxes, interest charges, dividends, and gains or losses from liquidation of investments or disposition of land, buildings, and equipment ought to be treated separately from the determinants of operating net margin. These items are, from the viewpoint of management, outside the main stream of operations; they represent distributions of income rather than determinants of it. Though it is true that stockholders' shares in net income must be viewed as the residual after such income adjustments or distributions are given effect, it is also true that the measure of basic managerial effectiveness is more properly the figure that results from regularly productive operations before tax adjustments (which may be applied to an income figure quite different from the operating net margin) or the costs of financing are taken up. The figure which serves to

Figure 5-1
PROFIT PLAN, FIRST QUARTER AND REST OF FISCAL YEAR 19—

	April	May	June	First Quarter	Rest of Year	Total for the Year
Sales						
Units	5,000	5,250	6,000	16,250	43,750	60,000
Dollars	$100,000	$105,000	$120,000	$325,000	$875,000	$1,200,000
Deductions	2,200	2,310	2,640	7,150	19,250	26,400
Revenue	$ 97,800	$102,690	$117,360	$317,850	$855,750	$1,173,600
Expense						
Standard cost of goods sold	$ 65,000	$ 68,250	$ 78,000	$211,250	$568,750	$ 780,000
Selling costs	15,000	16,400	20,000	51,400	133,750	185,150
General administrative costs	9,500	9,600	10,500	29,600	92,000	121,600
Total expense *	$ 89,500	$ 94,250	$108,500	$292,250	$794,500	$1,086,750
Operating net margin	$ 8,300	$ 8,440	$ 8,860	$ 25,600	$ 61,250	$ 86,850

* Includes Depreciation, $7,920 ($2,640 per month). Expense might also include variances from standard cost.

evaluate the overall program summarized in the profit plan is the operating net margin.

When the profit plan has been put together by the budget officer's staff, it will appear something like Figure 5–1. The figures in this summary will be supported by detailed schedules and analysis, so that there will be some basis for deciding whether or not the operating budgets summarized in the profit plan are acceptable in terms of overall profitability.

REVIEW AND POSSIBLE REVISION

If the profit plan is acceptable, the process of budget preparation has achieved one of its purposes, and it may be approved by top management (along with the departmental schedules which were the basis for preparing it). Usually, however, full approval is withheld until the effect of budget plans may be seen in terms of financing transactions and their effects.

If the profit plan is not an acceptable pattern from the viewpoint of profitability, the question that must be answered is, What can be done to improve this result? Here the budget officer may help managers to replan by working out on paper what might be expected if certain changes are made. This is not easy, because the first estimates were based on what were considered to be the best possible courses of action. The methods that can be used (postponing development or research expenditures, for example) usually involve sacrificing future advantages for the sake of current income. But whatever chance there may be for such improvement must be followed out with care, so as to achieve the desired result without too great a risk of bad effects.

After such review and revision as may be indicated, top management will at least be satisfied that the profit plan is as good as can be expected. This result is essential to the success of the budget program.

THE FINANCIAL SUMMARY—THE CASH BUDGET

Cash Management

To continue operating, a business must produce results (revenue) that are greater in amount than its current period costs (expense). Revenues and expenses are settled at one time or another by money transfers; but one of the salient features of modern business is the lag of money flows created by credit. A business must be able to make payments when required to avoid embarrassment, and it necessarily must carry cash balances to take up the differences between receipts and payments over time. But cash balances ought not to be larger than necessary, for idle cash earns nothing.

Some companies have staff officers who manage the cash balances of all divisions and offices; they transfer idle cash to places where it is needed, and they make short-term investments of seasonal surpluses. They may also maintain relations with banks and other financial institutions, so that when the company needs more cash than is supplied from operations, the needed funds can be had with a minimum of delay and cost. Obviously, such activities rely heavily on budget forecasts of cash flows in and out of the various parts of the business, as well as for the firm as a whole.

Forecasting Collections

To manage cash effectively, it is desirable to forecast collections from customers (the most important source of funds) as well as to project disbursements that will arise from resources and services to be acquired. It is usally easiest to forecast collections from gross sales rather than from net revenues after uncollectibles, discounts, and other offsets. Although revenue offsets may be related in terms of percentages to sales billed, they are not distributed this way through time. Discounts, for example, will affect cash receipts via a lag of ten or 20 days from sale; uncollectibles, returns, and allowances have no relation to cash flow except that those amounts will not be collected at all. Outward freight may require cash *payments* at time of sale, such amounts to be collected when the customer's account is settled.

LAGS IN COLLECTION. If all sales were made on uniform 30-day terms and if all discounts, freight items, and so forth were settled precisely as intended, the sales billed in one month would be a close approximation to the collections of the following one. This would not be exact, however, because of variation in the weekdays included in individual months and the consequent variation of collections. From this point of view, there is merit in a 28-day accounting period over a monthly basis; each "period" would begin on the same day of the week, and each period would contain exactly four weeks. Some companies follow such a plan, although the practice is not universal.

But customers do not all remit on the same pattern; some pay up even before the discount period is over, but others are slow, even to the extent of abusing credit privileges. It is necessary, therefore, to make some allowances for this in forecasting cash receipts from customers. Data to make this possible may be collected by making statistical analyses of collection lags and patterns. Such studies may be only partially accurate, for the experience patterns may shift seasonally or cyclically; but they can be used to make short-run predictions.

MECHANICS OF ESTIMATING COLLECTIONS.   To illustrate the pattern of calculation, assume that the Model Company's experience indicates that for any month's sales, 60 percent will be collected within the discount period (terms 2 percent 10, net 30). Three quarters of these (45 percent of the total sales) will be collected within the month of sale, the rest in the following month. An additional 10 percent of the sales (on which discounts will have lapsed) will be collected within the month of sale (the company is strict about discounts). A further 25 percent of sales will be collected in the month following the sale and 4 percent in the second month after sale, leaving 1 percent as uncollectible.

Since any budget period must begin with some existing receivables, the first part of the working paper (Figure 5–2) will be concerned with them. In this case, the January sales were $80,000, of which only the $800 uncollectible items remain. February sales of $90,000 would have left $4,500 of receivables on the books, of which $900 would be uncollectible; the other $3,600 will be collected in April— the second month following sale. The actual figure is $4,800, which is not surprising. The $300 excess is expected to be collected in April. March sales of $95,000 would normally have left $42,750 of receivables— (1) 1 percent uncollectible, 4 percent to be collected in May; (2) 25 percent not subject to discount but collectible in May; (3) 15 percent subject to discount and collectible in April. The totals that would have remained on the books from March sales would normally have been $42,750; the actual amount is $200 more. But the $42,950 actually left at the end of March will be collected: $14,500 in April less $290 discount; $23,700 in April without discount; $3,800 in May. The other $950 will remain uncollectible at the end of the period. Now, the combined calculations show at this point how much will be collected during April, May, and June from the $48,550 of receivables actually on the books at March 31. The reader will note that the work sheet shows the discounted collections on a line separate from those not subject to discount.

The normal pattern of allocation may be applied to the expected sales for April, May, and June. In June, however, the carry-over of 15

Figure 5–2

WORK SHEET FOR FORECASTING CUSTOMER COLLECTIONS (ALL FIGURES IN DOLLARS)

Month of Sale	1 Gross Amount of Sales	2 Receivables Left for Settlement	3 Discounts Allowed	4 Collected in April	5 Collected in May	6 Collected in June	7 Uncollected at June 30 Gross	8 Uncollected at June 30 Allowance	9 Uncollected at June 30 Net
January	80,000	800					800	800	0
February	90,000	4,800		3,900			900	900	
March		14,500	290	14,210					—
	95,000	28,450		23,700	3,800		950	950	—
Total, first quarter	265,000	48,550	290	41,810	3,800		2,650	2,650	—
April	100,000	60,000	1,200	44,100	14,700				
		40,000		10,000	25,000	4,000	1,000	1,000	—
May	105,000	63,000	1,260		46,305	15,435			
		42,000			10,500	26,250	5,250	1,050	4,200
June	120,000	72,000	1,080			52,920	18,000	360	17,640
		48,000				12,000	36,000	1,200	34,800
Total, April, May, June	325,000	325,000	3,540	54,100	96,505	110,605	60,250	3,610	56,640
Total, both quarters	590,000	373,550	3,830	95,910	100,305	110,605	62,900	6,260	56,640

percent of the month's sales subject to discount leaves $18,000 of sales with outstanding discounts of $360 still to be taken in July. Thus, the "allowance" column includes not only an allowance for uncollectibles but also for "open" discounts. A check on arithmetic is provided by the fact that the sum of items in columns 3, 4, 5, 6, and 7 should equal the amount in column 2. This is true for every line as well as for totals.

The aggregate collections for the three months of the second quarter are shown as grand totals of columns 4, 5, and 6. Figures for the position budget, showing uncollected receivables of June 30, appear as grand totals of columns 7, 8, and 9. Actually, of course, there will be write-offs of receivables to reduce the amounts in columns 7 and 8; perhaps the only significant figure for the position budget is the sum of column 9.

Forecasting Disbursements

Cash payments that will be required for the forthcoming budget period may be estimated in various ways, depending on conditions. For the simplest situation, we may estimate disbursements by referring to the department cost schedules, where we will find different operating charges presented in detail. Any given operating charge or cost item may be evaluated to determine its effect upon cash position. Some of these are settled in the same month they are incurred— charges for repairs made by outside concerns and some items of supervisory or other regular monthly payroll are examples. But some of the operating charge items will be paid for at least in part in the month following their incurrence. Some payroll costs, traveling expenses, commissions, supplies, and so on will be carried over from one month to another as accruals. In many cases it is possible to establish simple estimates for these—such as deferring half the monthly total to show the disbursement for a semimonthly payroll. Some costs (such as materials cost, when inventories are maintained at a constant level and terms are 30 days net) may be listed as cash disbursements in the month following their incurrence. A few disbursements (dividend, rent, insurance) may be payable quarterly, and some, such as property taxes, may be paid semiannually or annually. Still other items (such as depreciation and depletion or patent amortization) require no recurring payments; the payment for such items occurred when they were acquired.

To use operating charge figures as cash disbursements assumes that such goods and services are acquired only as needed, so that the inventory position remains unchanged. This is not always the case, although it may be close enough to the truth to cause not too much error in the forecast of disbursements. But if the cash forecast is to be accurate, some attention ought to be given to fluctuations of materials and supplies inventories.

The operating charges for materials and supplies may be adjusted by adding the increases (or subtracting the decreases) in materials and supplies inventories calculated in terms of the change in quantities times the expected net purchase cost per unit. This is done for each month in the budget period; the estimated purchases may then be lagged appropriately.

THE PURCHASES BUDGET AS A MEANS OF FORECASTING DISBURSE-MENTS. A better way to approach the problem of allowing for inventory changes in materials and supplies is to make use of the purchases budget described in Chapter 4. This forecast will combine the materials and supplies requirements for the whole firm by item and sources of supply, and it will also take account of planned expansion or reduction of various inventories. The purchases budget may involve delivery arrangements and contractual settlements which will specify the cash needs much more definitely than the operating charges shown in the departmental cost schedules. The preparation of the purchases budget thus simplifies the forecasting of cash disbursements.

ALLOWING FOR WORK IN PROCESS AND FINISHED STOCKS INVENTORIES. If disbursements were to be forecasted from expense data, a similar correction would have to be made to add increases (or subtract decreases) of *work in process or finished goods* inventories to the expense estimate. This is not necessary when operating charges (as shown in departmental cost schedules) are used to forecast cash requirements. All inventory increases are automatically included in the forecast of operating charges; any decrease in inventories is taken into account, if operations are scheduled at a rate lower than the rate of transfer or delivery. Therefore, the operating charge department schedules may be used as described above, rather than to separate current from various kinds of lagged disbursements in preparing the cash forecast.

USE OF PAYROLL BUDGET TO FORECAST DISBURSEMENTS. The forecasting of cash payments may be made much easier if the operating charge data are summarized properly. One aspect of this is the use of the purchases budget to combine similar items, so that inventory and sources of supply may be considered more realistically than by viewing each department's needs by themselves. A similar situation may exist with respect to payrolls. Summarizing all weekly-rated factory payroll costs from the department schedules makes it possible to forecast the amount of payroll to be settled on given dates and to establish accrued amounts as aggregates for the plant as a whole. Semimonthly payrolls should be accumulated separately (not merged with weekly or monthly totals); this permits homogeneous and accurate forecasts of disbursements for each class. Two observations are important here—when data are homogeneous, only one set of calculations need be made for each class (such as semimonthly payroll); therefore, summarization saves work. But any lack of homogeneity makes the resulting projections subject to error. Putting all fringe benefits (holiday pay, vacation pay, group insurance, and Social Security contributions) together will result in a most inaccurate cash forecast, because these items range from weekly to annual payments, with some of them erratic.

However, this merely emphasizes the merit of using a payroll budget to establish disbursements. Combining the labor requirements for the various departments in the firm has a real merit in maintaining and encouraging full utilization of skills by transferring workers between departments wherever a full schedule may be achieved in this way. Further, personnel programs for recruitment, training, or promotion may be encouraged, and this makes it possible to do a better job of having people available for assignments when they are needed. In addition, the payroll budget permits a full review of personnel costs and fosters more accurate projections as to various fringe benefits or labor related costs. It also makes it easier to calculate payroll disbursements.

"OTHER OPERATING CHARGES." Setting up procurement budgets and using these to forecast disbursements for materials, supplies, and various payroll related costs leave only a part of the disbursements for operating charges to be forecasted from the departmental schedules. Such charges as utility services, outside contracts for maintenance and repair, travel, association memberships, or miscellaneous minor items may be readily combined and dealt with in totals. Utility services would generally be paid for in the month after the costs were recorded, even though the actual meter readings would cover a somewhat different period than the fiscal month used by the company. Most of the other costs would be disbursed in the month in which they were incurred. Property taxes are typically paid semiannually, and depreciation and amortization do not require disbursement.

LIABILITY ACCRUALS. Thus far, we have ignored the fact that a company will ordinarily begin the budget period with certain accruals of accounts payable for materials and supplies, various contracts, and other items. There will be obligations for payrolls and related items, property taxes, utility bills, and so forth. These must be included in the forecast of disbursements.

ASSET ITEMS. The procedures already enumerated will have set up all the expected disbursements to cover the recurring items of operating charges, except items subject to depreciation and amortization. A few short-term items (like insurance and rentals) may be paid in advance for a year or more. The summarized amortizations from monthly journal entries will indicate how much of these costs will be absorbed during the budget period. This will not only provide data needed for the expected position statement but will check also on the expenditures for prepayments and capital assets. The prepayments and capital items expenditures occur at erratic intervals; they will usually be added to the operating disbursements as totals carried from subordinate working papers to the cash budget summary.

CORPORATE DISBURSEMENTS. In addition to the payments that will be required to settle obligations for operating costs and asset acquisitions, there are outlays that must be made by the company as an institution. These will include interest changes on borrowed capital, federal or state income taxes, and the dividend distributions to holders of preferred or common shares.

To the extent that interest arises from continuing debt—such as a bond issue or an intermediate-term loan—the interest charges can be computed from past data. Interest bearing obligations or short-term notes used in financing operations or asset acquisitions will have to be added into the corporate disbursements schedule. From the profit plan data, the interest charges, and other relevant information, the expected payments on income taxes may be computed. Dividends expected on preferred and common shares would also be tabulated in this part of the cash forecast.

The Summary Cash Budget

In order to obtain an overall view of the flow of cash in the firm by the budget period, all the cash transactions are summarized in a summary cash budget; collections from customers, operating disbursements, payments for asset acquisitions, and corporate disbursements are put together to be able to see the aggregate effects of cash transactions for the period. This will take a form like that in Figure 5–3.

The summary cash budget is the means of focusing attention upon the short-run financing problems of the firm. A failure of cash receipts to cover disbursements indicates the need for financing; an excess of receipts over disbursements may indicate the desirability of retiring indebtedness or of putting otherwise idle funds to use. The question of dividend disbursements may be much more sensibly dealt with if the management has a clear picture of cash needs for various purposes. The summary cash budget should be prepared by the budget officer's staff, using comments and suggestions of the chief financial officer of the company. In a larger company, the summary cash budget may be submitted to a finance committee for discussion, amendment, or approval. In any event, the summary cash budget shows the top managers and directors of the company the effects that will be felt in cash position during the budget period and how these will be dealt with.

Illustrative Cash Budget

By referring to Figure 5–3, it can be seen that in this case the financial program raises no crucial problems. Although cash on hand will decline from $23,400 to $15,470 during the quarter, the firm will be able to meet all current obligations as they mature month by month. The assumption involved here, however, is that the spacing of events within a month may be ignored—that is, that receipts and payments *within* the month will occur so as to cause no timing problems. This, of course, is not necessarily true. It could be that collections from customers would arrive only in the latter days of the month, while disbursements may be required earlier. Presumably, these calculations would be more precise if made to match by weeks or by days, to ensure the availability of cash for every obligation. However, this ideal is hardly worth much attention, for the errors in forecasting the precise date of invoices and collections would be too great to add much validity by the use of the short time interval. This

Figure 5–3

SUMMARY CASH BUDGET, FIRST QUARTER, FISCAL YEAR 19—

	Payable March 31	Obligations Incurred for Quarter	April	May	June	Payable June 30
			Disbursements			
Materials and supplies (purchases budget)	$ 7,600	$109,600	$ 27,100	$ 33,200	$ 37,700	$ 19,200
Payrolls (payroll budget)	9,250	184,200	56,400	59,300	62,700	15,050
Building repairs		1,800		1,200	500	100
Power, heat, and light	600	3,200	900	1,100	1,300	500
Insurance		1,300	1,300			
Property taxes	600	600				1,200
Travel	300	950	300	350	400	200
Miscellaneous services	200	6,700	2,100	2,200	2,500	100
Income taxes	5,200	10,480	5,200			10,480
Recurring items, total	$23,750	$318,830	$ 93,300	$ 97,350	$105,100	$ 46,830
Building and equipment additions		$ 82,000			$ 82,000	
Mortgage interest		4,000		$ 4,000		
Mortgage retirement		13,000		13,000		
Totals	$23,750	$417,830	$ 93,300	$114,350	$187,100	$ 46,830
Long-term equipment loans					$ 80,000	

Summary	April	May	June	Quarter total
Net cash required	$ 93,300	$114,350	$107,100	$314,750
Cash on hand first of month	$ 23,400	$ 26,010	$ 11,965	$ 23,400
Collections from customers	95,910	100,305	110,605	306,820
Total cash available	$119,310	$126,315	$122,570	$330,220
Cash balance forward	$ 26,010	$ 11,965	$ 15,470	$ 15,470

(from Figure 5–2)

does not deny that companies do try to speed up collections and to manage cash outflow for optimum effect. But for budget estimates it is seldom feasible to forecast daily or weekly cash flows. In the present case there is a sufficient balance of cash in sight to be reasonably sure that there will be no problem of great importance on this score.

Cash Deficits

Sometimes the cash budget will show a cash deficit in one part of a budget period but a net positive balance at a later time. This might easily happen during a period in which an increase in volume of business occurs. The lag in revenue collections may cause cash receipts to fall behind operating outlays, because the bulk of operating charges require fairly prompt cash settlement. After the higher volume level is established, the cash deficiency disappears because collections will have built up to the same relative level as operating outlays. A situation like this exhibits a clear case for short-term borrowing, because the budget shows not only when and how much of a loan will be needed, but also when and how the cash will materialize to pay off the loan. It is easy to see why banks often require budget estimates to support loan applications.

Sometimes the cash needed to cover disbursements is more than can be acquired from regular operations, and short-term or long-term financing may be required. The summary cash budget will show how much is needed during the current period and whether it can be repaid. Sometimes a longer forecast may be made to see how long the loan may be needed or whether the funds required ought to be raised as permanent loan or equity capital.

Excess Cash Balance

Just as there may be cash deficits revealed by the summary cash budget, there could be substantial increases in cash balances. This may occur when the volume of operations slows down, reducing the need for cash outlays to cover lower (variable) costs, even while collections continue from the earlier high rate of sale. Cash may also build up from reduced disbursements related to the reduction of inventories or other ways of operating from assets acquired earlier— such as the use of facilities already paid for, depreciation of which represents a current cost of operation that does not require cash.

Buildups of cash balances are cause for some concern, because they require that some use should be made of the excess funds. In a seasonal business this may be a recurring problem, requiring the purchase and sale of short-term investments within the year to make use of otherwise idle cash.

Generally, however, managers have a good many uses for excess funds; modernization and improvements are often possible, as are other opportunities for investment or advantageous retirement of debt. In the rare case in which no such opportunities exist, any excess cash should properly be returned to shareholders, who could then make their own reinvestment decisions.

Budgeting Fund Flows

The preparation of a detailed set of cash estimates is sometimes considered too tedious for practical purposes, and managers (or budget officers) may look for some way to simplify this proposition. The argument for this is that short-term loans are usually easy to arrange and that one has to depend on them in any case. Thus, it is argued that a forecast of net working capital changes would be sufficient to meet the need which the cash budget would supply.

The fund flow approach avoids working with intraworking capital transactions, such as the collection of receivables or the payments for purchases or payroll. Rather, the financing pattern would be developed in the way in which a typical statement of funds is prepared. An illustration of such a forecast appears in Figure 5-4.

Figure 5-4
PROJECTED FUND FLOWS, FIRST QUARTER, FISCAL YEAR 19—

Operating net margin *		$25,600
Deduct interest charges †	$ 4,000	
Income taxes †	10,480	14,480
Net income to shareholders		$11,120
Add financing effect of depreciation *		7,920
Working capital increase from operations		$19,040
Reduction of mortgage principal	$13,000	
Equipment additions $82,000 ‡		
Less specific financing 80,000 ‡	2,000	
Reduction in working capital		15,000
Net increase in net working capital		$ 4,040

* From profit plan.
† From cash payments budget or special calculations.
‡ From capital expenditure requests.

A summary statement such as that in Figure 5–4 may be prepared quite easily from the profit plan and other related data. It does serve in a general way to check the profit plan with respect to financing effects. But it does not give very much useful information beyond this general view. If the fund flows summary replaces the summary cash budget and the computation of collections from customers, it is not possible to establish much about the financial position to be expected, and the whole problem of the management of working capital—as related to relative investments in inventories or receivables or the short-term financing patterns to be employed—is sidestepped. This may be advantageous for practical reasons. But the primary use of budgets is to raise issues in advance that will have to be dealt with in a forthcoming period; this, so far as cash flows are concerned, the fund flows analysis simply does not do. Thus, there is good reason to establish the summary cash budget as a test of the overall program of operations, to raise on paper the issues that will have to be met.

THE POSITION BUDGET

Projecting the financial position of the firm at the end of the budget period is easily done when the profit plan and the summary cash budget have been prepared. Most of the data that make up the projected financial position have been established and may be collected from the various working papers. A review of the major items will make clear how these figures are obtained.

Cash

The summary cash budget will show the amount of cash that will be on hand when the transactions of the period have been completed, once the necessary financing has been arranged. The final figure as approved by financial executives and top management is merely carried into the position statement.

Receivables

The net amount of receivables that will remain uncollected at the end of the budget period was established in computing the collections from customers. Not only does the working paper used to project collections show the net uncollected receivables at the end of the period, but the adjacent column shows the amount of open discounts and the amount of estimated uncollectibles that would be in the gross receivables at that date. These figures are thus available for the position budget.

Inventories

In the preparation of the purchases budget, the inventory position was evaluated and stated in detail. For the position budget it is only necessary to summarize the materials inventory data from the purchases budget.

Work in process and finished goods stocks were calculated in preparing expense data for the profit plan. Departmental operating charges were converted into expense figures by adding or subtracting the amount of inventory change. These would probably be stated in terms of standard unit costs, but they could be handled on a current-average-cost basis or even on a first-in-first-out or last-in-first-out basis. In any event, the data are already available in the expense computation.

Prepayments

Among the items that were taken into account in converting operating charges to disbursements there appeared the credit for amortization of those costs which did not require disbursement. Also, among the asset acquisition items in the disbursements analysis appeared the advance payments made for the renewal payments or new contracts written for insurance, rents, or other similar items. The renewal and new contract payments, added to the balances current at the beginning of the budget period, less the amounts amortized during the period, yield the amount of prepayments in the position budget.

Plant Assets and Intangibles

The amount of assets of this type usually changes only slowly. The initial balances will be reduced by the amount of depreciation or amortization shown in the working paper used to convert operating charges to disbursements. New acquisitions will appear in the asset acquisitions schedule of the summary cash budget or in the "funds applied" section of a fund flow projection. Thus, both the gross and net amounts assets subject to depreciation, depletion, or other amortization will be available for inclusion in the position budget.

Current Debt

Figures established when the purchases budget was converted to a disbursement basis will establish accounts payable for materials and supplies. Liabilities for utilities and miscellaneous charges will be taken up from the disbursements schedules. If the payroll budget is established as a disbursement schedule, the amounts of accrued payroll, federal and state payroll taxes, and vacation pay and other fringe benefits will appear in those working papers. Accrued interest, federal tax liability, and dividends payable will show in the summary cash budget calculations, or they could readily be established from the data used there.

Long-Term Equities

These, like plant assets, change only slowly over time; but the advent of new long-term financing would have been noted in the summary cash budget. The initially outstanding long-term debt and the preferred and common share investment would be adjusted for the additions or retirements shown in the summary cash budget or the fund flow projection. And the shareholder equity in retained earnings would be adjusted to include the operating net margin from the profit plan, as well as whatever income distributions that may have been involved.

To show how these data would be combined in a specific case, Figure 5–5 exhibits the comparative position budget related to the illustrative material presented earlier. The reader will find it interesting to trace the figures in this exhibit back to those data presented in the other summary budgets.

Test Function of the Position Budget

It should be easy to see that the position budget affords a clerical check on the entire process of budget preparation. Even though we have not tried to maintain a double-entry pattern for the recognition of transactions, the position statement at the end of the budget period must still balance if all the data have been handled properly. Thus, an oversight or omission in the summarizing process would tend to be found in the test of equilibrium.

But the position budget affords a broader kind of test for the budget program as a whole. Management may look at the expected position budget as a means of visualizing the accomplishments of the budget period. If the program as planned tends to put strains into the company situation (for example, overinvestment in receivables, inventory, or plant; excessive current or long-term debt, or other kinds of imbalance that a position statement can contain), management can see this in summary terms and can rework the program to avoid the

Figure 5–5

COMPARATIVE POSITION BUDGET, 3/31 AND 6/30, 19—

	3/31	6/30	Net Increase (Decrease)
Current assets			
Cash in bank	$ 23,400	$ 15,470	($ 7,930)
Accounts receivable (net)	45,610	56,640	11,030
Inventories	25,920	49,330	23,410
Prepayments	490	1,100	610
Total current assets	$ 95,420	$122,540	$27,120
Current debt	$ 23,750	$ 46,830	$23,080
Net working capital	$ 71,670	$ 75,710	$ 4,040
Plant and equipment (net)	$216,700	$290,780	$74,080
Total net resources	$288,370	$366,490	$78,120
Mortgage on plant	100,000	87,000	(13,000)
New equipment loans		80,000	80,000
Common shares	150,000	150,000	
Retained earnings	38,370	49,490	11,120
Total capitalization	$288,370	$366,490	$78,120

undesirable results. Often, the forward view of the expected financial position three months hence may call attention to conditions that can still be adjusted or corrected. Such a view may precipitate a more careful study of long-range plans or even a reconsideration of some aspects of company objectives.

The important thing to be noted here is that management may still change any part of the program as it may desire. A changed emphasis on various sales or operating patterns, a reduced pattern of expansion of investment, a different plan of financing or income management— all may be considered and worked out to see whether they will yield the desired results. Once this has been done to the satisfaction of management, the biggest task for the forthcoming period has been done. We have decided what is wanted and how it should be done, and we have a fairly good idea of why this is so. The fact that so many alternatives have been considered in the various stages of budgeting means that we have been exposed to a wide variety of patterns and choices. We have had the opportunity to weigh and try all these choices which seem advantageous, and the entire plan has been stated in unequivocal terms. If this plan is carried out as outlined, the results to be obtained are clear; the plan may be put into operation without undue concern about the outcomes—the only problem is to see that the plan is carried out in the way it has been stated.

REVIEW, REVISION, AND ADOPTION OF THE BUDGET

In prior discussion, it was suggested frequently that budgets are subject to review and revision at various places and by various individuals. This is as it should be, for no one manager can plan even his own operations so that his plan will be optimum from every viewpoint. Since management is a collective rather than an individual affair, it is necessary that such review and revision be a part of budgeting. However, two observations must be made. First, there should be some positive action which serves to bring revision and adjustment to a close; it is essential that the budget should be "adopted" or otherwise given official status. This is typically the act of top management or the budget committee in a formally communicated notice.

Second, the budget ought not to be adopted or otherwise formalized unless the revisions that may have been made are cleared back to the initiators of departmental schedules. This is not to give a veto power to those who must carry out the program, but to make sure that they are aware of what has been revised and *why* those revisions were made. Granted that a manager prefers to run things his own way if possible, there is no reason why he will not accept adjustment or even curtailment of his own ideas if he is given a chance to see the need for such restrictions. There should be ample means of communication and adequate discussion and explanation of all budget revisions and adjustments, to maintain that *esprit de corps* which is essential to effective management.

SUMMARY

This chapter has presented the content and the method of preparation of the budget summaries, the profit plan, the financing budget, and the position budget. All companies do not prepare these, and some of them are prepared only partially; the summary cash budget may be supplanted by the broader and less detailed fund flows projection. Full and detailed approach to the preparation of budget summaries results in financial statements "in the future tense," as it were. The position budget in such a case may be as detailed as its counterpart that will appear as a financial statement at the end of the period. But even if the overall process of summarization is cut somewhat short for practical reasons, the profit plan is essential to the budget program as a means of carrying the proposals for the future period to the point of applying the overall test of profitability. In an enterprise economy, there is no better way to evaluate the effects of the programs proposed.

There are still some issues that need to be considered with respect to budget enforcement. These are discussed in Chapter 6.

QUESTIONS

1. What are the purposes of budget summaries? Why can't these purposes be served by departmental budgets?

2. If managers are to prepare and to have responsibility for budget execution, why should they be subjected to review by the budget office, if they have consulted with their superiors and subordinates in preparing their budgets?

3. Certain kinds of adjustments usually are taken into account in carrying sales budget data into the profit plan. What are these adjustments, who should make them, and how are they established?

4. Why, if there are detailed budgets for all operating costs, is it necessary or desirable to use standard cost of goods sold in the profit plan?

5. Why does the profit plan emphasize operating net margin rather than net revenue for the year? What items are involved in this computation, and how do these enter the overall evaluation of the budget summaries?

6. If the budgets are subject to revision as a whole or in part by top management (the budget committee), why aren't the estimates simply prepared at that level? Does it not discourage a department manager to have his budget altered by fiat?

7. What is "cash management"? Do small companies need to do this? How would they do it?

8. What data are required to convert revenue figures into periodic cash collections? How would such data be accumulated?

9. If a company prepares a cash budget showing receipts and disbursements in detail, what, if any, purpose is served by a fund flows summary?

10. What are the major sections of a position budget, and where does each of the figures come from? Of what use is the position budget to the firm? Would it be useful to outside creditors?

11. Evidently, much time and effort (which cost money) go into the preparation of budget estimates. This is presumably justified by the use of the budget as a control device. But what can be said for the position that if the summary budgets were immediately thrown in the wastebasket when they were approved by top management, they would be worth more than they cost?

12. The financial statements of this company for the first quarter of this year are given on pages 137–138.

The company's sales for the first quarter have been January, 20,000 units; February, 30,000 units; and March, 40.000 units. Terms of sale allow a 2 percent discount from the list price of $3 per unit for payment by the end of the month of sale, net 60 days. Collections average as follows: 30 percent of each month's sales is collected during that month (less 2 percent), 60 percent is collected in the month following, 8 percent is collected in the second month following sale, and 2 percent is uncollectible.

The relations between factory costs and the rate of output are indicated in the income statement. Inventories of finished goods, however, are always valued at a "normal cost" of $2.10 per unit. In January 20,000 units were manufactured; in February, 40,000; and in March, 50,000.

Expected unit sales for the next quarter are April, 60,000; May, 50,000; and June, 25,000. The unit selling price of $3 will be maintained. The factory production schedule calls for an output of 60,000 units in April, 40,000 units in May, and 30,000 units in June.

Materials are purchased in quantities required for production, but a minimum inventory of materials sufficient to produce 10,000 finished units is always maintained. Materials are paid for in the month in which they are purchased. Cost of supplies and miscellaneous variable and fixed factory costs are paid in the month in which those costs are incurred.

Direct labor, indirect labor, and supervision costs make up the total factory payroll. These, as well as selling commissions and expense and all administration costs, are paid half in the month in which they are incurred, half in the following month. Power bills are paid in full in the month after they are incurred. Property taxes are paid semiannually: a disbursement of $6,000 will be made for these at the end of June. Insurance and depreciation will not require disbursements during the forthcoming quarter.

The company has an arrangement by which it may borrow up to $20,000 for not longer than 60 days from the Roger County Bank; the bank charges interest at 6 percent per year on such loans, payable at the maturity of the loan. A cash balance of $3,000 must be maintained. No more cash is to be borrowed than is necessary to maintain this balance, but loans are made only in full thousands of dollars.

ILLINOIS NOVELTY COMPANY
Balance Sheet
March 31, 19—

Cash in bank		$ 3,580	Factory wages and salaries	$ 23,500
Accounts receivable	$ 94,200		Sales commission and expense	10,000
Allowance, uncollectibles	5,400		Administration costs accrued	2,000
Inventories, materials	10,000	88,800	Accrued property taxes	3,000
Finished goods	42,000	52,000	Accounts payable (power)	2,000
Prepaid insurance		2,100		
Plant and equipment	150,000		Capital stock (8,000 shares)	240,000
Allowance, depreciation	3,000	147,000	Retained earnings	12,980
Total assets		$293,480	Total equities	$293,480

ILLINOIS NOVELTY COMPANY
Income Statement
Quarter ended March 31, 19—

Revenue			
Gross billings (90,000 units at $3 each)		$270,000	
Less: Provisions for uncollectible accounts	$5,400		
Discounts taken by customers	1,620	7,020	
Revenue from operations			$262,980
Expenses			
Factory cost of goods (110,000 units produced)			
Materials appropriated to production		$110,000	
Direct labor costs incurred		88,000	
Factory overhead			
Variable costs: Indirect labor	$11,000		
Power	4,400		
Supplies, misc.	6,600	22,000	
Fixed costs: Supervision	6,000		
Property taxes	3,000		
Depreciation	3,000		
Insurance	300		
Miscellaneous	2,700	15,000	
Total factory costs incurred		$235,000	
Less: Unsold inventory of finished goods		42,000	
Factory cost of goods sold		$193,000	
Selling expenses (which vary proportionately with sales)		45,000	
Administration costs and expenses (fixed)		12,000	
Total expenses			$250,000
Net margin from operations			$ 12,980

Prepare:

(a) An estimated income statement showing the effects of the expected transactions for the second quarter.

(b) Forecasts of collections from accounts receivable by months and of disbursements by months.

(c) A summary cash statement, showing the amount of bank loans and the repayment of them; this statement should also show the expected cash balance at June 30.

(d) An estimated balance sheet showing the expected financial position of the Illinois Novelty Company at June 30.

13. The president, sales manager, and plant superintendent of the Athol Corporation held a conference to decide an issue of selling prices. The sales manager insisted that the company's prices were too high,

and he proposed an across-the-board reduction of 10 percent in prices. This, he said, would put the firm on a sounder basis competitively; furthermore, he was certain that such a step would increase the physical volume of sales by 20 percent from the level of the past year.

The plant superintendent said that the constant pressure to reduce costs was affecting the morale of his foremen, and he thought that the company ought not to lower prices but to raise them, so that it would not be necessary to increase volume, as the sales manager suggested. He had been able to avoid overtime work, he said, but the pressure for output at low cost had made it hard to complete work in time to meet customer "promise dates." There had been some late deliveries, and occasionally some slight reduction in quality of product; fortunately, the quality reduction had not occasioned any customer complaints. He feared that if the sales manager's proposal were to be adopted, he would have to operate the plant overtime, go to a second shift operation, or acquire more equipment to be able to handle the greater volume. He thought a general increase in the price of products of 5 percent would improve the prospects of profit; he did not think the physical volume of sales would fall more than 5 percent from present levels if prices were increased by 5 percent.

The president reviewed the earnings report for the previous year, which had just been released by the firm's auditors and was unquestionably correct. This report is reproduced below.

The sales manager immediately pointed out that the unit cost of the product was $5.28; $3.30 for production, $0.825 for selling, and

ATHOL CORPORATION
Report of Earnings
Year ended December 31

Sales revenue 200,000 units at $5.50			$1,100,000
Production costs (for 200,000 units):			
(a) Materials, direct labor, power, etc.		$440,000	
Depreciation, superintendence, etc.		220,000	
Total production costs		$660,000	
Selling costs:			
(a) Commissions, shipping, etc.	$ 55,000		
Salaries, depreciation, etc.	110,000		
Total selling costs		$165,000	
General administrative costs:			
(a) Supplies, postage, etc.	$ 88,000		
Salaries, fees, etc.	143,000	$231,000	
Total expense			$1,056,000
Operating net margin			$ 44,000
Income taxes			17,380
Net earnings retained			$ 26,620

$1.155 for administration. The indicated net margin of 22¢ per unit would represent, for 20,000 additional units sold, an increase in net profit of $4,400. Even after income taxes at 39.5 percent ($17,380/$44,000), there would be $2,460 added to earnings retention. He felt that the change in unit selling price would easily be offset by the fact that unit costs are lowered as volume increases.

The plant superintendent did not make a cost forecast, but he said that he thought the costs labeled (a) in the earnings report would be 5 percent less with the 5 percent reduction in output. This would effect a cost savings of $29,150. ($440,000 + $55,000 + $88,000 = $583,000; this × 5 percent = $29,150.) This would easily offset the effect of the small increase in unit cost from lower output levels, even after the income tax was figured in.

The president was uncertain about which of these positions was correct. He did not like to change prices or output schedules without good reason. Changed prices might bring repercussions in the market; the plant had been designed by consulting engineers for a capacity of 200,000 units per year. He was tempted to suggest that the entire situation be left unchanged for the time being.

6

BUDGET
ENFORCEMENT

Once the budget has been prepared and adopted in final form, one may say that the directive aspect of management has been expressed in the budget summaries and schedules. There remains, however, the task of carrying these plans into fruition, seeing that what has been established and agreed upon is actually done. This phase of budgetary control could be referred to as an "enforcement" operation—putting into force the actions that have been determined. "Enforcement," however, appears somewhat too strong a term to indicate what happens in the carrying out of managerial plans—the process must be cooperative if it is to be successful, because people are led, not driven.

Yet there is a phase of budgeting which does have to do with getting results, and that is our present concern. This consists (as has been previously suggested) of arranging for "feedback," so that interpretations and corrections may be made. The collection and interpretation of operating data for this purpose is discussed here.

THE NEED FOR BUDGET COMPARISONS

The planning aspects of budgeting are advantageous to management, for they are effective ways to obtain broad understanding and cooperation in collective decision making. If budgeting were stopped when the budget was completed for the firm, it would have achieved real benefit in producing coordinated and integrated plans, thought through for the whole enterprise. But the test of a plan is whether or not it works; this involves comparisons of actual results with expectations.

Of course, there are several reasons why results may not agree with expectations. There is always some random variation arising from unidentifiable causes; it is possible that changes may occur in underlying conditions or that there are errors in the measurements that are reported. But, in general, when there are real differences between expectations and results, there are two basic explanations: (1) The plan as set up was not followed in such a way as to achieve desired results or (2) there was some error in making the plan in the first place. In either case, management has a job to do. The failure to follow out a plan is the result of poor administration—faulty communication, untrained or incompetent personnel, poor quality of materials or equipment, or other inadequacies. These conditions ought to be corrected in the interest of the better performance that would result. But if the plan itself is a poor one—not well thought out or based upon unrealistic premises—managers can use the feedback information to discover what was wrong with the plan. Thus, in either case, the comparison of planned and actual performance may increase management's understanding of its problems. Every operation needs to be planned to be reasonably sure of results; every plan must be followed up to see that operations stay on course.

Accounting Feedback

The accounting system performs one of its most important functions in collecting data concerning all internal and external transactions of the firm. These data are reported back through an impersonal information system which serves as an observation device. The classification and analysis of accounting information will show whether or not the planned results are being obtained. By setting out reports which parallel the organization chart against the plans and schedules made by departmental executives in preparing the budget, accounting provides the kind of information needed for budget administration.

Each report of operations will be of interest to not only the manager in charge of that particular area but also his superior, because they are both concerned with the comparisons which appear there. Careful interpretation of the differences between planned and actual results should indicate *why* the operations have not occurred according to plan, or in what way the plan was deficient or inadequate. Both the manager and his superior may discuss and decide what ought to be done to achieve a closer agreement between goals and performance.

This process of analysis and correction will be applied to many different activities—ranging from sales, through manufacturing, selling, or general administrative departments or units, including such staff activities as personnel, purchasing, maintenance, and research and development—to include every management or service unit in the firm. The reports and comparisons will vary somewhat in form and content, but they will be similar in that they point out and analyze variances, so that managers may be better informed and more effective in their administration.

EXAMPLES OF BUDGET COMPARISONS

Sales Reports and Analyses

There are many ways in which sales data may be reported and analyzed; the forms and procedures actually used by a company will depend on the number of products, the scope of the market, and the way in which the sales function is organized. Similarly, the comparison period may vary with conditions or with managerial preferences. Various bases of analysis may be used. There are reasons for compiling data about customers, credit terms, size of city, or other factors; the most common procedure is to combine product and territorial classifications, because sales activities are frequently organized in that way. A sales report which uses this approach to budget comparisons appears in Figure 6–1.

A TYPICAL SALES REPORT.   The report in Figure 6–1 shows data for only one territorial division, subclassified by four lines of product. Both physical units and dollar amounts are given for sales, and these data are accumulated by weeks within a four-week budget period. The reader may recall that this is one variety of reporting arrangement among others. A monthly comparison could have been used or even a quarter or semiannum, but the advantages of weekly data accumulated over a four-week comparison interval are fairly clear in this situation. The report also separates two basic factors in the over and under budget results: physical volume and prices. Comparing actual prices and volume with expected prices and volume produces measures of change from these factors. This indicates something about the way in which operations have gone, which mere totals cannot show. The report might be expanded to include year to date or prior year figures; these might highlight trends if the comparisons are carefully drawn. In some cases, the report would also include such statistical data as the number of calls, orders taken, miles traveled, or other measures of sales effort; generally, however, the report as prepared by the accounting department would not include data collected by the sales division for its own purposes. But there could be information about unfilled orders and the reasons for them, provided

Figure 6-1

SALES ANALYSIS, EASTERN TERRITORY, APRIL 1–28, 19—

Product Details

Week ended	Product A		Product B		Product C		Product D		Totals
	Units	Dollars	Units	Dollars	Units	Dollars	Units	Dollars	
April 7	1,000	$ 6,000	2,200	$17,800	8,200	$ 32,800	5,000	$10,000	$ 66,600
14	800	$ 4,800	2,400	$19,200	9,400	$ 36,000	7,000	$14,200	74,200
21	400	$ 2,200	2,100	$15,600	9,300	$ 35,800	8,000	$16,100	69,700
28	1,200	$ 6,500	1,800	$15,000	10,200	$ 40,000	9,000	$17,900	79,400
Total four weeks	3,400	$19,500	8,500	$67,600	37,100	$144,600	29,000	$58,200	$289,900
Budgeted	4,000	$24,000	8,000	$64,000	37,000	$148,000	30,000	$60,000	$296,000
Over budget †			500	$ 3,600	100				$ 3,600
Under budget †	600	$ 4,500				$ 3,400	1,000	$ 1,800	$ 9,700
Volume variance	600 × $6	($ 3,600)	500 × $8	$ 4,000	$100 × $4	400	1,000 × $2	($ 2,000)	($ 1,200)
Unit price and price variance	(26.5¢)	($900 *)	(4.7¢)	($400 *)	(10.2¢)	($3,800 *)	.7¢	200 *	($ 4,900)
	* 3,400 × $.265 appr.		* 8,500 × $.047 appr.		* 37,100 × $.102 appr.		* 29,000 × .7¢ appr.		($ 6,100)

† Combined variances.

by production or shipping departments and transmitted by the budget office. Sales reports might also be set up to include sales expense data, such as travel and communications costs and salaries or commissions for the period.

The form here presented is thus not a model; each company will have reason to prefer one approach over others. But the results of sales operations must in any case be reported back to the person in charge of this territory and to his superior as well. Study and discussion of these data by these interested parties should produce action to bring actual results closer to budget goals or to indicate how and why the budget expectations need to be revised.

Operating Cost Reports

Budgets for operating departments generally take the form of a list of operating charges—costs of carrying on the planned activities. As these departments go about the tasks they are supposed to accomplish, the accounting system will as a matter of regular procedure collect the actual charges for costs incurred. Periodically, these costs may be compared to the budget figures to see how closely they conform to the expected results.

The budgets were prepared by each department head, and the reports are set up to match those departmental schedules. Thus, the reports concerning the costs of operation will follow the patterns of "responsibility" accounting, in which the classifications of data are set up to match with the decision making powers of the person in charge of each department. One way of doing this is to maintain a multicolumn ledger account for each department or reporting unit, with columns for each of the major cost or revenue classifications about which decisions can be made. This account may carry other data to reflect facilities provided or services used; however, such costs should be shown in a separate section from the controllable costs for which the department head is responsible. A typical form of this kind—which could serve for both the recording and reporting functions—is shown in Figure 6–2.

The report shown in Figure 6–2 shows a typical breakdown of costs incurred, matched with budget allowances for each of the major cost categories. The noncontrollable charges are included to show the manager how much it costs to supply those facilities used in his operations. Although these costs are not large in this case, they do at least indicate that such costs exist and that they need to be borne in mind, even though the manager cannot control them by his own decisions.

Figure 6–2 *

DEPARTMENTAL COST REPORT, DIVISION X, DEPARTMENT 29, APRIL 1–APRIL 29, 19—

Reference or Document No.	Personal Service Costs			Materials and Supplies Costs			Other Controllable Costs			Noncontrollable Charges				Totals
	Direct	Indirect	Premiums	Other Fringe Costs	Direct Materials	Supplies	Power, etc.	Maintenance	Other Outside Services	Supervision	Interest and Depreciation	Building Space Charges	Other Miscellaneous	
XP 1734	4,254	879	230	814						400				6,577
XM 1217					7,514	328								7,842
XJ 719							1,112	649						1,761
XD 2717									359					359
XG 1112											1,320			1,320
XG 1113												641		641
XG 1174													128	128
XP 1735	4,216	864	120	822						400				6,422
XM 1218					8,021	179								8,200
Totals	8,470	1,743	350	1,636	15,535	507	1,112	649	359	800	1,320	641	128	33,250
Budget	8,200	1,500	350	1,580	15,600	400	1,000	700	300	800	1,320	650	100	32,500
Over	270	243	—	56		107	12		59	—	—		28	775
Under					65			51				9		125

Net variance, total .... over 650

* All figures in dollars except reference and document numbers.

It will be noted that the charges arise from typical accounting system procedures. The reference or document number gives some indication of the source of the item charges. XP 1734 and 1735 are the regular biweekly payroll entries; "premiums" refers to overtime compensation, shift differentials, efficiency, and other bonuses which do not vary in close conformity with the rate of operations. "Other fringe costs" refers to holiday and vacation pay, Social Security taxes, and employer contributions to insurance or profit sharing plans. Reference numbers XM 1217 and 1218 refer to regular recapitulations of materials and supplies requisitioned from stores. Internal transfers such as charges for power and maintenance ("billed" against Department 29 by the service departments) are covered by a "journal voucher" transfer, XJ 719. (Invoices from other companies arise as disbursement items, which appear on a separate disbursement voucher form.) Similarly, the XG 1112, 1113, and 1174 items are General Administrative Costs, prorated to this division and department.

The departmental cost report form may actually be a copy of the departmental cost account, and the totals may be forwarded from one period to another. This would permit comparisons on a "year to date" basis if desired.

In this case, the budget differences are small; yet it is clear that some deviation does exist. It is of interest that the excess usage of supplies more than offsets the saving in direct materials; this could be merely an error in accounting classification. The "under" item for maintenance cost may indicate only that some maintenance work had been deferred, perhaps because of schedule problems. Or it could be that the extra "outside services" charge represents some maintenance work which was done by an outside repairman—perhaps because the needed repair had to be done while the regular maintenance men were busy with other pressing things. There are various reasons why costs may be higher or lower than plans allowed for, and only those who follow the operations closely are in a position to know what those reasons are. All the accounting system may be expected to provide is an overall check on the items charged to cost. But this overall check serves to raise significant questions.

Interpretation of Variances

It is almost certain that actual figures will not agree precisely with the budget, for many factors intervene, only some of which can be estimated in advance. And the report just described can only show the *aggregate* difference between budget and actual costs. It is quite conceivable that the small reported net differences actually contain much larger amounts that have offset each other. For example, direct labor costs may have been $150 more than they should have been on one day and $142 less than expected on another. The totals in the report would be affected by only the $8 difference. This suggests that a shorter reporting period would disclose such variations, which could then be brought under closer scrutiny and control. The question is, of course, how much variation is really to be expected, or how much of a difference is really significant.

PERCENTAGE VERSUS STATISTICAL MEASURES. Sometimes there is a temptation to view the aggregate variance in terms of its percentage relation to the expected amount. For instance, the direct labor cost variation is $270; related to the budget of $8,200, this is only a little more than 3 percent. The indirect labor variation is 16 percent of the budget figure. Such percentages can be useful, but they do not necessarily indicate importance of the variance. Every operation or activity has some inherent variance due to chance causes—factors which are individually undeterminable, but which in their aggregate effect are of some importance. The only way to determine how much variance is significant is to apply statistical tests to the detailed data. The reader is referred to works on statistical method for elaboration of this idea.

As a practical matter, managers (and budget officers, too) will tend to develop a sense of proportion and insight as they review budget variances related to familiar activities. The knowledge of a process can be used to suggest causes not only for a single variance item but for groups of them; in some situations this may be more productive than mechanical analysis alone. A process that involves cutting materials out of sheets or lengths may show larger scrap losses even though efficiency is maintained, if for some reason purchased sheets or lengths may vary in size or other characteristics. A favorable variance in materials prices may really mean only an overzealous purchasing agent searching for bargains. Untrained workers may cause not only excess labor time, but materials wastage, machine breakdowns, and other things. When some conditions change, an overemphasis upon mechanical efficiency may affect product quality, with disastrous results that do not show in manufacturing variance accounts. It may be more productive for managers to look at more than one variance at a time in the search for causes and tendencies. An alert budget officer can encourage and develop perspective on the part of the managers by encouraging them to use variances not only as mechanical instrument readings but as aids to navigation—indications which call forth ingenuity and perspective. To do this, he needs to develop a little of this attitude himself.

FLEXIBLE BUDGETS

Ideally, the budget plan specifies the particular combination of departmental activities which fits anticipated conditions in optimal fashion. This is as it should be, for any plan should aim at the best possible solution to overall problems. But there is a certain rigidity in such a program which may make it awkward. When the productive activities of a manufacturing department are planned for 5,000 units of product per month, what happens if delays in the receipt of materials, machine breakdowns, or other unforeseeable events upset the program? Suppose the delay reduces the output to 4,000 units for the month; would the comparison of actual costs with the budget be very meaningful?

To illustrate this situation, consider the comparison in Figure 6–3. The budget differences in Figure 6–3 are misleading, because the

Figure 6–3

BUDGET COMPARISON, UNADJUSTED FOR OUTPUT DIFFERENCES

	Actual Cost, 4,000 Units	Budget, 5,000 Units	Difference
Direct materials	$20,000	$24,000	$4,000 under
Direct labor	11,800	15,000	3,200 under
Indirect and fringe labor	4,000	5,000	1,000 under
Power, supplies, etc.	6,300	8,000	1,700 under
Supervision and other fixed costs	8,200	8,000	200 over
Totals	$50,300	$60,000	$9,700 under

budget for 5,000 units is not comparable to the actual operating level of 4,000 units. The reduction in output would have the effect of lowered variable costs, which does not appear in the budget figures as given. All the comparisons except the one for Supervision and Other Fixed Costs are inaccurate, because the variable costs would have been expected to fall when the rate of operations declined. Hence, the budget should be adjusted to fit the rate of operations actually encountered. Then the figures would appear as in Figure 6–4.

The first four cost items would be compared with a budget of 80

Figure 6–4
BUDGET COMPARISON, FLEXIBLE BUDGET, ADJUSTED FOR OUTPUT

	Actual Cost, 4,000 Units	Budget Adjusted to 4,000 Units	Difference
Direct materials	$20,000	$19,200	$800 over
Direct labor	11,800	12,000	200 under
Indirect and fringe labor	4,000	4,000	0 —
Power, supplies, etc.	6,300	6,400	100 under
Supervision, fixed costs	8,200	8,000	200 over
Totals	$50,300	$49,600	$700 over

percent of the original amounts, since these variable costs would have been expected to fall to that level, along with the drop in output. The fixed cost of $8,000 would be left at that figure. The total difference is much less than in Figure 6–3, because the effects of the volume reduction have been removed. But the detailed variances are more meaningful, because they reflect the difference between what did happen and what should have happened when output was reduced.

Suppose, for instance, that the manager had attempted to save direct labor cost by using lower grade workers at lower rates of pay. The saving would appear to be $200; but the effect of this or of a reduction in Power, Supplies, Etc. may have been to increase materials costs because of worker errors that arose from inexperience or poor working conditions. This kind of analysis is possible only when the budget estimates refer to conditions and levels of output that were actually experienced. The overincurrence of direct materials cost and fixed costs and the lower than expected direct labor and power and supplies costs are differences which would be controllable and traceable to the department manager's decisions. This kind of comparison is much more useful than the original budget differences in Figure 6–3.

Because of the effect just seen, it is common practice to adjust the budget figures for expected changes in volume of operations, recognizing that variable costs differ from fixed costs in this connection. This procedure of separating variable costs and showing what they ought to be at different activity rates is called flexible budgeting, because the budget figures can be made to conform to changes in the rate of activity.

Refinements of Flexible Budget Procedure

The approach to budget analysis that has just been suggested is a simple one, based on the notion that costs are either variable with units of output or fixed for any level of output. This approach does improve the usefulness of budget comparisons—in effect, it restates the budget figures as they would have been if our original forecast of volume and costs had been more nearly correct. But this may be extended with real benefit if we are willing to refine the basis for our computations.

VOLUME MEASUREMENTS.   It is easy to reckon volume of operations in terms of output; but this is not the most effective way to do so. When one considers the way in which costs are incurred, it is obvious that output is the result, not the determinant, of costs incurred. The factors that really determine costs are *input* factors; materials costs are the result of the number of units of material put into process, labor costs result from time spent in doing things, and facilities costs result from setting up the operations in a certain way. Thus, the amount of cost incurred should not be interpreted in terms of output, unless the relation between input and output is constant.

EFFICIENCY AT VARIOUS ACTIVITY LEVELS.   The level at which operations are carried on may have definite effects upon efficiency. If the low level of output occurs because of changes in schedule beyond the control of the manager, the schedule change should not be allowed to produce budget variances for which he will be held accountable. In the present case it may be that although materials usage at the 5,000 output rate is 2 pounds per product unit, this efficiency of materials usage might be unattainable at a smaller output level. The materials required at 4,000 units of output may be 2.02 pounds per product unit. Then a 4,000 unit month would have required 8,080 pounds of materials, which at $2.40 per pound would be $19,392 instead of $19,200 as shown in the first line of Figure 6–4. The more accurate budget allowance would then produce a variance of only $608 instead of $800.

Similarly, the direct labor required for 5,000 units per month might be 6,000 man hours, but 4,000 units of product might require 4,900 man hours—a slightly less efficient situation. Then the direct labor cost comparison should be $11,800 of actual cost against a budget of $12,250 (4,900 × $2.50 per hour)—a saving of $450. The net sum of the direct materials and direct labor variances would be only $158, instead of the $600 difference that appeared in Figure 6–3. Relative efficiency in the use of resources has its effect on cost results.

BUDGETING FROM ACTIVITY RATES.   A reasonably close control of indirect costs may often be achieved by using "activity rates" to forecast or interpret the indirect costs as a group. This approach disregards individual cost behavior patterns and allows the manager a bit of leeway in the interest of a simpler procedure. Thus, all indirect variable costs might be forecasted as a group (in the situation described above) at the rate of $2.17 per direct man hour. If the relation between indirect variable cost and man hours operated is linear, the rate is the "slope" of the line of relationship, which may be calculated as the originally budgeted $5,000 indirect and fringe labor, plus $8,000 of power, supplies, etc. (a total of $13,000), divided by the man hours required at the originally forecasted level of operations. At the 4,900 man hour level (4,000 units of product require 4,900 man hours), the budget allowance would be $10,613. In the present case, the $10,300 of costs incurred would be compared with the budget allowance of $10,613 (see Figure 6–2 or 6–3) or $4,000 + $6,300, leaving a variance of $313 under budget. This is larger than the $100 under budget variance in Figure 6–3 because the allowance is figured at the *actual* number of man hours that should be required for the given production schedule (4,900) instead of the 4,800 man hour level implied by the earlier presentation.

It should be observed that this rate computation cannot be used for fixed indirect costs. Fixed costs are forecasted for a time period during which they will be the same for a wide range of operations. The fact that a fixed cost rate can be used to make estimates of the cost of maintaining idle facilities is a matter of standard cost accounting which lies outside the field of this discussion.

SEPARATE RATES FOR MAN OR MACHINE ORIENTED COSTS. It is possible that the assumed linear relation between total variable indirect costs and the man hour or other base may be distorted by differences among man or machine oriented costs. That is, some variable indirect costs may be more closely associated with man hours, while others are correlated with machine hours of operation. In such a case it may be desirable to use separate rates to forecast and interpret these different groups of cost. In the illustration used here, the man hour rate applicable to indirect and fringe labor costs could be set at $.83 ($5,000 ÷ 6,000 man hours) per direct man hour, and the budget allowance at 4,900 man hours would be $4,067. If the 5,000 unit budget had called for 2,000 machine hours, the machine hour rate would be $4.00. The budget allowance for, say, 1,620 machine hours would then be $6,480. This would produce budget variances of $67 under and $180 under for the two parts of the cost associated with man and machine operations. Note that by this procedure one may make forecasts which take into account the need for relatively higher inputs per unit of product when operations are scheduled at less than normal capacity.

The use of budget allowances based on man or machine rates to control variable indirect costs is a useful way to deal with a complex situation. It does permit some discretion on the part of the manager as to whether a particular item of overtime or extra supplies may be added to offset some other cost in the interest of overall efficiency. It also tends to focus attention on the broader aspects of control rather than on minor differences which may be hard to explain or avoid. The choice of method reflects to some extent how much freedom the manager may have to use his own discretion within limits set by more general budget allowances.

Extensions of Flexible Budgeting

This discussion has proceeded far enough to make it clear that any cost may be forecasted within reasonable margins if we relate our forecast to those things that really affect the cost. An attempt to follow this notion a bit further is interesting. While this may be a somewhat complicated problem, one might express a revenue forecast as

$$R = f(p, q, e, s, \ldots).$$

That is, revenue is a function of the unit price, the quantity that can be produced, the elasticity of demand, the amount of sales effort, and other factors, such as credit liberality, the degree of quality maintained in the product, the sales of other products, and so on.

Similarly, we might express the cost situation as

$$L = (m, r, e, t, \ldots),$$

which is to say that the cost of labor (in some activity unit) is a function of the number of man hours used, the rate of pay, the "efficiency" complex (age, training, experience, and attitudes of workers), and the time factor (day of week, time of day, season of the year), as well as other variables, such as the quality of materials, the condition of machinery or other tools, the temperature or humidity, and so on. If one could specify such functions precisely, using measured (and continuous) relationships among these variables, a forecast would be merely a matter of calculation. This idea is not altogether a pipe dream. Within the constraints of existing knowledge, this is precisely what flexible budgeting aims at and—in rough and ready terms—what it achieves in the real world even now. The range of error is perhaps wider than we would like, and the variables may be hard to recognize and control, but the flexible budget is an attempt to make such forecasts and achieve such results.

But the notion we have presented is capable of greater application than we have yet suggested; some companies are already engaged in such applications. Given a fairly extensive "bank" of experience data and a willingness to try out some statistical techniques, it is possible to establish "estimating equations" which can be used to forecast in various degrees of detail. When a statistical analyst and a computer are together put to work on this problem, one can use such equations in a combined budget model, which would include simple patterns like $I_o + P_1 - I_1 = U$ (the familiar inventory, purchases, and usage relation) or an expression like

$$\phi = \sum_1^n (m_i \, 1_i) + \sum_1^n (q_i \, p_i) + \sum_1^n [m_i \, (v + f)].$$

This equation states the total standard cost of products completed during a period in terms of conventional measurements, using a man hour rate for indirect cost allocation. Another such pattern could be set up as follows:

$$M_n = \frac{\sum_1^n (m_i)}{n} = a \, (n)^r, \text{ or } \log M_n = \log a + (\log n) \, (r).$$

This is a "cost improvement function" stating that the cumulative unit variable labor time at the level of n units of output is expressed as the initial unit variable labor time (a) multiplied by the number of units (n) raised to a power of the cost reduction ratio (r), which is the percentage decline in unit variable labor time, per percentage increase in output. The logarithmic transformation is merely another way to write out the relationship. This is merely one way of saying that a given task will tend to become more efficiently performed as the operators "learn" to do it. The relation is empirical—that is, its truth depends on whether or not it fits the facts of a situation—but such patterns may be valid and useful.

With a full set of such relationships, it is possible to forecast with a high probability of success. If the forecasts are truly precise, any variation is (theoretically) an index of error or of the presence of an unrecognized variable. Thus, the day-to-day feedback may be matched with the forecast in terms of an adjustment for not only output and input variations, but all other factors allowed for in the model. Variances are then really an indication of something not allowed for, and thus worth looking into for each one of the controllable variables as well as the other (external) factors.

A computer program may be applied to whatever new data or revised estimates become available. This makes it possible for any change in conditions or shift in relationships (such as the substitution of less costly but less efficient labor) to be brought into the budget forecasts. It is possible to build into the model such decision mechanisms as linear programming, which will establish the optimum allocation of resources for a given set of such conditions.

But this approach may be carried even further. It is possible to see what would happen under purely hypothetical conditions—that is, to answer questions about what would happen if . . . . It is even possible to try out novel arrangements between variables. If we could write (or are willing to assume that we can write) an equation to show how a department manager would react to "loose" or "tight" budget constraints, we might be able to estimate how much pressure is worth putting on to reduce costs. This is, admittedly, a bit "far out"; it may not be unattainable or even have doubtful merit, but it does suggest a real potential for managerial control. The future of such things is not our present concern, but it is an intriguing subject.

RESPONSIBILITY FOR VARIANCES

When budget reports show differences between planned and actual performance, there arises the issue of how strictly the budget should be enforced. It is not always easy to say just which variance is most important or to establish causes for individual variances. Such questions can be answered only by those close enough to the operations to be able to associate conditions and events with the cost or revenue data as analyzed. If the sales of certain products in specified territories behave in a way that was not expected, the person that should do something about it is the one in charge of those territories. Hence, it is not possible for the budget officer or his staff to do much more than report variances in as meaningful terms as possible. Where subclassifications or other analysis can be made, this should, of course, be done. But the comments, if any, about budget reports and comparisons should arise first from the manager whose decisions and operations are involved. Questions are implied by every budget comparison, the answers to which must await at least the study and comments of the manager. Typically, the reasons for conditions that require correction are less important than the choice of means to correct them, and this is a line management responsibility, not a task to be attempted by staff personnel.

But the budget office staff and the accounting and statistical analyses that can be made should be made available to managers who ask for further data or supplementary studies. The factors that lie behind a sales decline in a given territory may require more than observation and comment of the management. The budget officer and his staff need to be ready and willing to search for data or to apply methods of study which will help managers deal with their problems.

The decisions which arise from budget reports and analyses are those of management. The reports which go to departmental managers and their immediate superiors—and the summary tabulations which are sent to division chiefs or top executives—are information devices, not criticisms or directives. Staff functions such as accounting and budgeting are intended to assist, inform, or otherwise serve the line management. The nearest approach any budget officer can make with respect to operating management decisions is to give advice. Even this, for obvious reasons, is a move into dangerous territory where every staff officer needs to watch his step.

SUMMARY

This chapter has presented some of the issues involved in carrying out the budget program to report the actual revenue and costs against the budget forecasts. The need to make comparisons of this kind has some effect on the forms and procedures used in accounting. Classifications of cost and revenue are based on the managerial organization chart, with special emphasis on those items whose amount may be changed by managerial decisions. Responsibility accounting is a necessity if budgetary control is to be effective. One form of revenue account was presented to illustrate some aspects of this kind of accounting and reporting.

A typical form of departmental cost account, arranged in terms of managerial responsibility, was discussed, and a copy of this account was used to set up comparisons between the actual and the planned figures for each cost item.

The differences between budget and actual figures (variances) require interpretation. The mere amount of such variances is not always the way to measure their importance. Statistical analysis may be necessary to establish the natural variability of given items, by using frequency distribution analysis to measure statistical variance. But this is sometimes developed by managers intuitively. Budget officers must be ready to use statistical tools if needed.

The notion of flexible budgeting was developed at some length to indicate some of the ways in which budget variances could be interpreted and controlled. Refinements in this area need to be tailored to fit specific conditions.

In the last analysis, however, the administration of budgets is a management responsibility which is related intimately to the decision making authority. For this reason, no budget officer can expect to do more than inform and assist line managers in carrying out budget plans. The adjustments and corrections which may be required can be facilitated sometimes by further analysis in accounting or statistical terms, but the function of the budget officer is at best an advisory one. The budget is a powerful tool; the budget officer may be a careful analyst and a sympathetic and constructive adviser; but the responsibility for results is never transferred from those first charged with it—those who manage the operations.

CONCLUSION

We end this study of budgets and budgeting quite close to the same thoughts with which we began. Managers decide how a business shall operate and who shall be responsible for what part of the work that must be done. They decide when, how, and why things shall be; the budgeting process is only a way to give expression to managerial decisions in concrete terms. This quantification and systematization is but a furthering of the kind of thinking and action which good managers employ. Thus, the division of responsibility which allows the budget officer to handle the systematic details of this procedure is itself only one phase of managerial activity. But the fact that budgets enable (or even force) managers to be more specific in their plans and more objective in enforcing them, makes management a more effective process; by careful reckoning against a charted course, one may more easily reach a desired goal.

QUESTIONS

1. Using a flexible budget control system on a departmental basis, the Malibu Company has its internal operating reports prepared on a four-

week basis 13 times a year. During the ninth such period this year, the estimated production to be assembled in one of the departments was 50,000 units, and expected activity for this output was expected to be 10,000 direct man hours. The departmental cost items and the basis on which they were estimated appeared in the budget as follows:

Direct labor	$17,150	Variable with direct man hours
Materials and parts	23,400	Variable with units of product
Indirect labor	3,050	$550 plus 25¢ per d.m.h.
Supplies	1,900	19¢ per d.m.h.
Power and light	1,430	$30 + 14¢ per d.m.h.
S.S. taxes and insurance	783	3.6% of payroll cost
Overtime premiums	200	$100 at 5,000 d.m.h. + 2¢ per additional d.m.h.
Idle time	150	1½¢ per d.m.h.
Supervision and clerical	1,200	Fixed staff
Repairs to equipment	400	Judgment of supervisor
Depreciation	850	Straight line time on cost
Property taxes and insurance	325	Fixed
General overhead	2,140	Prorated on basis of payroll Includes personnel, administration, and other departments
Total budget, Period 9	$52,978	

In the middle of the period, a small fire shut down operations for a few days. At the end of the four-week period, actual operations had been at only 8,000 d.m.h., and only 39,000 units of product had been produced. The operating charges for this period are shown below.

Direct labor	$14,330
Materials and parts	17,950
Indirect labor	2,550
Supplies	1,600
Power and light	1,150
S.S. taxes and insurance	657
Overtime premiums	50
Idle time	120
Repairs to equipment	1,100
Supervision and clerical	1,200
Depreciation	850
Property taxes and insurance	340
General overhead	1,920
Total	$43,817

Make up comparisons between the original budget and the actual costs, showing individual variances in columnar form. Also show flexible budget allowances based on 39,000 units and 8,000 direct man hours with variances in the final two columns of the form.

2. One division of the Kuppermettel Products Company produces an item that is used in assembling a number of the company's other products. Capacity of this division is stated as 3,000 product units per week of 40 hours. A normal week would involve 2,700 machine hours of operation and 3,600 direct man hours. Materials required would run about three pounds per product unit.

At the beginning of a four-week budget period, direct labor wage rates were $2.50 per hour; direct materials price was 50¢ per pound. Other costs are budgeted on various bases: indirect labor (which consists mostly of materials handling) at 15¢ per pound of materials used; indirect materials are estimated to run 30¢ per direct man hour; machine power and repairs should run 30¢ per machine hour. Fringe labor costs are expected to be 25 percent of direct, indirect, and supervisory labor; this last is fixed, $200 per week. Depreciation accrues at $150 per week, and property taxes are figured at $100 per week. Building occupancy costs are partly fixed ($100 per week), partly variable (6¢ per direct man hour), and partly seasonal; the annual total of seasonal costs is $1,920, of which one-fourth is expected to be incurred during the forthcoming period.

(a) Prepare a budget for this division, assuming that the normal level of output is maintained for the entire four-week budget period.

(b) Defining variable costs as those which move up and down with the rate of production, set up a four-week budget for an expected level of 10,000 units of product for the period.

(c) During the actual operations of the budget period, the actual output was 10,000 units. The average wage rate, however, was $2.60 per hour, the materials price averaged 52¢ per pound, and there were 8,020 machine hours operated. The actual costs were the following:

Direct labor	$33,800
Direct materials	16,120
Indirect labor	4,700
Indirect materials	3,890
Fringe labor costs	9,780
Power and repairs	2,460
Building occupancy	1,730
Property taxes	400
Depreciation	600
Supervisory labor	820
Total charges	$74,300

Assuming that wage rates, material prices, depreciation, and property taxes are not controllable by the division manager, prepare budget comparisons for this period.

(d) Contrast the results in making judgments about efficiency of the operations by using budgets (a), (b), and (c) above.

INDEX